LATINOS
AND
U.S. FOREIGN POLICY

LATINOS

AND

U.S. FOREIGN POLICY:

Representing the "Homeland"?

Edited by

Rodolfo O. de la Garza

and

Harry P. Pachon

ROWMAN & LITTLEFIELD PUBLISHERS, INC.
Lanham • Boulder • New York • Oxford

#44426724

E
184
.S75
L3685
2000

ROWMAN & LITTLEFIELD PUBLISHERS, INC.

Published in the United States of America
by Rowman & Littlefield Publishers, Inc.
4720 Boston Way, Lanham, Maryland 20706
http://www.rowmanlittlefield.com

12 Hid's Copse Road, Cumnor Hill, Oxford OX2 9JJ, England

British Library Cataloguing in Publication Information Available

Library of Congress Cataloging-in-Publication Data

Latinos and U.S. foreign policy : representing the "homeland"? / edited by
Rodolfo O. de la Garza and Harry P. Pachon.
        p.   cm.
Includes bibliographical references and index.
ISBN 0-7425-0136-1 (alk. paper)—ISBN 0-7425-0137-X (pbk. : alk. paper)
    1. Hispanic Americans—Politics and government. 2. United States—Foreign
relations—1989. 3. United States—Relations—Latin America. 4. Latin America—
Relations—United States. 5. Political participation—United States. I. Title: Latinos
and United States foreign policy. II. de la Garza, Rodolfo O. III. Pachon, Harry P.

E184.S75 L3685 2000
327.7308—dc21   00-042560

Printed in the United States of America

⊖™ The paper used in this publication meets the minimum requirements of American
National Standard for Information Sciences—Permanence of Paper for Printed Library
Materials, ANSI/NISO Z39.48-1992.

To Latino foreign service officers—may they serve the nation within and beyond the cucaracha circuit.

Contents

Acknowledgments

This volume was made possible through the generous support of the Ford Foundation and the Andrew W. Mellon Foundation. We would also like to thank the Public Policy Clinic of the Government Department at the University of Texas at Austin for its assistance. The research presented here has also benefited from the advice of Professor Jorge Domínguez of Harvard University and from the insights of its advisory board members: Salih Booker, director, Africa Program for the Council on Foreign Relations; Vishakha Desai, director, the Asia Society; Peter Hakim, president, Inter-American Dialogue; Manhaz Ispahani, program officer, the Ford Foundation; Yolanda Londoño, executive director, Houston Image Group; Rita DiMartino, AT&T director of Federal Government Affairs; and David Doerge, president, David G. Doerge and Associates.

PART I

LATINOS AND THE NATIONAL INTEREST

1
Introduction

Rodolfo O. de la Garza

The end of the Cold War has given rise to the charge that U.S. foreign policy is increasingly incoherent. The consensus built around the need to resist Communist expansion has been replaced by a foreign policy shaped to meet particularistic demands of domestic political actors. For our purposes, the relevant part of this critique is the charge that Latinos are among the new actors engaged in foreign policy and that their involvement threatens the national interest.[1] This allegation emanates from the belief that Latinos refuse to join the American mainstream and to abandon their historical political ties to ancestral homelands. The purpose of this volume is to offer an empirically grounded response to this indictment.

According to this anti-immigrant, antiethnic argument, the growth of the Hispanic population, fueled by the dramatic increase in immigrants seeking citizenship (U.S. Immigration and Naturalization Service 1999), will enable Latinos to have enough political clout to be effective advocates for policies favoring their countries of origin against U.S. interests. It is especially noteworthy that this allegation is voiced by widely disparate groups, ranging from nativists to distinguished scholars. Not surprisingly, it is also echoed by the American public at large. Peter Brimelow gives voice to the nativist perspective that is shared by individuals such as Pat Buchanan and organizations such as the Federation for American Immigration Reform. His anti-immigrant screed suggests that the United States is no longer that "interlacing of ethnicity and culture we call a nation," and he questions whether the American nation-state, "the political expression of that nation," can survive (1996, 232).

Brimelow's views are more subtly voiced in Arthur M. Schlesinger Jr.'s argument that state support of multiculturalism undermines national unity by encouraging and facilitating the rejection of the core values that define the American mainstream in favor of ethnic values and traditions that impede the Americanization of Latinos.[2] Schlesinger points to the Latino elite's support of bilingualism,[3] which he considers a "source of the fragmentation of America, another threat to the dream of 'one people' " (Schlesinger 1992, 107–110) to support his claim.

Samuel P. Huntington shares Schlesinger's assessment and explains its implications for foreign policy. He begins by asserting that Latinos "continue to adhere to and to propagate the values, customs and cultures of their home societies" (1996, 304–305). Thus, they are "being transformed from cultural communities within the boundaries of a state into diasporas that transcend these boundaries. State-based diasporas, this is, trans-state cultural communities that control at least one state, are increasingly important and increasingly identify with the interests of their homeland" (1997, 38). Consequently, their commitments to the United States are so tenuous that they will not support the nation during crises.

To illustrate his argument, Huntington describes a "highly improbable but not impossible" scenario regarding a future major war to which the Hispanic-dominated states of the southwestern United States are especially opposed. Hispanics in the region and the state governments they control say, " 'This isn't our war' and attempt to opt out on the model of New England in the War of 1812." (1996, 313–315). (It is noteworthy that Huntington does not mention that New England's opposition was influenced by the confluence of the deep historical, cultural, and familial ties its population had with England and the region's strong economic relationship to the homeland, none of which exist between Hispanics and China, the enemy in the hypothetical scenario.)

Huntington's argument also rejects the notion that the national interest should reflect the concerns of Latinos or any other interest group. In his view, the national interest transcends the sum of group interests. Consequently, he also suggests that ethnics such as Latinos do not have distinctive interests or perspectives that are relevant to the definition of the "national interest." He is therefore critical of efforts to involve Latinos qua Latinos in discussions regarding the definition of national priorities. Thus, he denounces an initiative of the Council on Foreign

Relations (CFR) intended to expand the involvement of Latinos and other minorities in the foreign policy process. The CFR's campaign has consisted of a systematic effort to increase the ethnic and racial diversity of its membership so that members will have the opportunity to participate in foreign policy debates. Huntington, however, describes these fledgling endeavors as "the ultimate symbol of the triumph of diaspora interests over national interests in American foreign policy" (1997, 40).[4]

Given that a wide range of U.S. opinion makers question Latino support of national interests, it should come as no surprise that the American public is equally dubious. In 1990, the American public ranked Latinos as less patriotic than Jews, Blacks, Asians, southern Whites, and Whites (Smith 1990). Hispanics were also ranked only above African Americans regarding their support for economic individualism, a core element of the American creed (Huntington 1991).

Elites and the general public, thus, doubt the depth of Latino patriotism, and they question the depths of Hispanic commitment to core American values. It follows, then, that they would be leery about having Latinos become actively engaged in foreign policy. How legitimate are such concerns? To what extent do the available data support or contradict this perspective? Do such concerns uniquely target Latinos, or are they comparable to how the nation responded to earlier waves of immigrants? These questions are the major focus of this volume.

Ethnics, Foreign Policy, and the National Interest

The nation has reacted with varying levels of concern to the role that ethnics might play in foreign policy. Predictably, the issue has been of greatest salience when, as was the case during World War I, the nation has had to deal with high levels of immigration and international conflict. The Japanese experience during World War II, however, illustrates that nativism can also fuel intense antiethnic reactions during war, even in the absence of high immigration.

The nation is again experiencing very high levels of immigration. Moreover, today's immigrants, most of whom are Latin American and Asian, are arguably more distinct from mainstream society than were the European immigrants of the 1890–1920 era. This new immigration is literally changing the face of the United States as well as broadening many of its cultural practices. This transformation, combined with historically rooted nativism and an undefined foreign policy paradigm, is giving rise to renewed concern about the role that ethnics will play in foreign policy. Given that immigration is likely to continue, these concerns may result in a new front in the ethnic struggle for full and equal access to all societal institutions.

Research on the role that ethnic groups have historically played in American foreign policy reveals several patterns (Ahrari 1987, DeConde 1992, Fuchs 1990). Most significantly, their involvement has not led to the kinds of schisms that give rise to separatist demands and cataclysmic struggles such as those in the Balkans, East Timor, or even Canada.[5] Second, American ethnic groups have continually attempted to become and remain full participants in the political process, and only after they have achieved that status have some groups tried to influence American foreign policy toward their countries of origin (Ahrari 1987).

Not all ethnic groups have mobilized to influence relations between the United States and their countries of origin, however. Two explanations may account for this third pattern. Some immigrants, for example, Swedes, Danes, and Norwegians, come from countries that have uncontroversial relationships with the United States; therefore, there is no need for them to mobilize around binational issues. Others are from countries whose relationship with the United States is so strained that mobilizing on behalf of the homeland would be futile. This may explain Italian American behavior during World War II (DeConde 1992, 115) as well as the low mobilization of Arab Americans since the Persian Gulf War of 1990–1991. Whatever the explanation, it is clear that not all immigrant communities, even when they are well organized, engage in foreign policy issues relevant to the *homeland.*

A fourth characteristic of ethnic involvement in foreign policy is that, even when they have the capacity to do so, ethnics are often timorous about engaging in foreign policy because it is an intrinsically high-risk enterprise. Although "politics stops at the water's edge" is an aphorism aimed at partisan politics, it has even greater portent for ethnic involvement with the homeland. The political consequences of placing or appearing to place the interests of countries of origin over those of the United States are even more dire than those partisans face if they try to advance their party's objectives at the expense of the "national interest." Thus, to be credible and avoid the suspicion of tepid Americanism or, worse yet, treason, ethnic elites involved with foreign policy are usually limited to engaging in issues that do not pit the United States and the "homeland" in zero-sum competitions. During World War I, for example, U.S. society viewed German American allegiances in zero-sum terms. Consequently, not only did German Americans have to sever their ties to Germany to avoid severe sanctions from U.S. authorities and society in general, but they were effectively silenced regarding the conduct of the war (DeConde 1992, 83–89).

Ethnic leaders have long worked within this constraint when they have attempted to influence U.S. foreign policy. During World War I, for example, Americans who supported England pushed for U.S. mobilization in support of the Allies on the grounds that it would benefit U.S. national interests, and they de-emphasized the extent to which their recommendations also supported England.

Similarly, Irish American leaders called for American neutrality on the grounds that this would serve the national interest, but they did not emphasize the belief that this policy would also serve Irish interests (DeConde 1992, 82–87). This is the same tactic American Jews have followed in their attempts to influence U.S. policies toward the Middle East. Win or lose, this type of involvement does not bring with it charges of disloyalty.

Other types of interest groups must also work within this constraint, even though they do not have to be as explicitly attentive to it. Thus, whether they reflect regional, economic, ethnic, or other types of interests, all actors who seek to influence foreign policy must claim that whatever policy they advocate is in the national interest. This includes even the traditionalists, who argue that "national interest" is a concept that is above politics and should be defined and implemented by a small subset of the nation's traditional elites.

In our judgment, such a claim is nothing more than a rationale for defending a particular set of policies that favor specific interests (Trubowitz 1997), as well as a justification for preventing the representatives of non-White communities, including Latinos and the American public in general, from engaging in foreign policy decision-making. As such, it is less valid than arguments that the national interest should be determined by means of political debate so that, ultimately, policies designed to defend the national interest accurately reflect the priorities of the electorate, just as all policies should.

Furthermore, given that the traditionalist argument runs counter to the fundamental democratic principles that govern this nation, it is our judgment that such a definition should be rejected in favor of one that defines the national interest as a political concept delimited through continuous competition among distinct publics representing a wide array of preferences based on regional factors, economic considerations, and ethnic considerations (Alterman 1998).

To be sure, there are characteristics common to all definitions of the national interest that no group may oppose and still remain politically legitimate, for example, defending the physical integrity of the nation's boundaries, protecting the nation from armed invasion and terrorist attacks, and maintaining national economic prosperity. The consensus surrounding these objectives, however, does not eliminate political conflict; it merely channels it toward how the objectives are to be realized. Are the nation's interests in the Middle East better served by supporting Israel or the Arab states? Does the Cuban boycott advance or retard the nation's economic and security interests? Is the nation's economic prosperity promoted by limiting legal and undocumented immigration rather than by opening the border to increased migration?

It is also important to note that some ethnic interests have influenced foreign policy for so many years that they are legitimate participants in the foreign policy process.

Indeed, as the English example from World War I illustrates, some ethnic interests are so entrenched that their role may go unnoticed (DeConde 1992, 82–83). Given this history, why is there such concern about Latino involvement in foreign policy?

Latinos and U.S. Foreign Policy

Clearly, the experiences of ethnic communities earlier in this century substantially resemble what Latinos face today. Sometimes, as in the case of Japanese Americans during World War II, ethnic groups were subjected to far worse treatment than Latinos have ever endured. Then, as now, ignorance, nativism, and racism fueled unfounded accusations and discrimination. Thus it is especially troubling that in the post–civil rights era such biases are once again coloring the lens through which Latinos (and other non-White immigrants) are viewed.

Mexican American loyalty, for example, is questioned, despite evidence of continuous and intense patriotism. In 1898, War Department officials questioned whether New Mexicans would support the war against Spain. An insulted Governor Otero responded by organizing a battalion that contributed to Cuba's defeat (Otero 1940). The *corridos* (folk ballads) that soon became part of New Mexican folk culture are evidence that the state's *Hispanos*[6] looked on their soldiers as heroes. Mexican Americans have similarly voiced great pride in their contributions to the military in general, and they are especially proud that during World War II they had the highest percentage of Congressional Medal of Honor winners of any identifiable ethnic group in the nation (Acuña 1988, 253).

Similarly, a 1990 survey compared Mexican American and Anglo support for core American values. Contrary to Anglo perceptions (Smith 1990), after controlling for demographic characteristics, the study found that "there are almost no statistically significant differences between the support Anglos and Mexican Americans express for economic individualism," and, more significantly, Mexican Americans who are U.S. citizens "express patriotism at levels equal to or higher than do Anglos" (de la Garza et al. 1996, 346).[7]

Evidence regarding language use and the commitment to learn another language also contradicts the claim that Latinos are reluctant to learn English and that this reluctance will lead to linguistic divisions that will balkanize the nation. Demographers have found that Latino immigrants learn English more rapidly than did European immigrants at the turn of the century (Stevens 1994). Furthermore, more than 90 percent of Mexican Americans, Cuban Americans, and Puerto Ricans agree or strongly agree that all citizens and residents of the United States should learn English. Latino linguistic behavior is consonant with these views. According to the 1990 census, approximately 95 percent of U.S.-born Hispanics are either monolingual English speakers or know English and

Spanish equally well, and even immigrants are somewhat more likely to know English than to be Spanish monolinguals (Tomás Rivera Center 1995).

There is also no evidence indicating that Latinos have become representatives for their countries of origin. For example, Hispanic members of Congress of Puerto Rican and Cuban origin and one Mexican American, Henry B. González, voted against the North American Free Trade Agreement (NAFTA), while the rest of the Mexican American delegation voted for it only after provisions were added that would benefit their U.S. constituents. In other words, the Mexican government's intense and well-financed effort to secure Latino support for NAFTA ultimately proved to be of little consequence (Eisenstadt 1997).

Mexican American policy preferences on other major issues such as immigration and border control also differ from those of the Mexican government (de la Garza and DeSipio 1998). These examples indicate that Mexican Americans are more likely to support policies opposed by the Mexican government than to advocate for them. Cuban Americans are even less likely to become advocates for the home government. As is well known, they are intransigent foes of the Cuban regime, and the Cuban American Foundation, the nongovernmental organization (NGO) most actively involved in Cuban issues, has been a major supporter of the U.S. government's anti-Castro policies. As U.S. citizens, Puerto Ricans cannot become advocates for a foreign government. Instead, Puerto Rico's major political question related to its relations with this country are whether it should remain a commonwealth or become a state.

It is also noteworthy that Latino foreign interests have focused on their countries of origin rather than on Latin America as a whole. Additionally, a 1990 survey found that the countries toward which Mexican Americans, Puerto Ricans, and Cuban Americans were most positive were the United States, followed by their respective countries of origin; curiously, they were also more positive toward Great Britain than toward any Latin American country other than their historical homeland. In other words, Mexican Americans were most likely to be positive about the United States and Mexico, and they were more positive toward England than toward Puerto Rico, Cuba, Venezuela, and Nicaragua (de la Garza et al. 1997, 409). Additionally, the evidence indicates that these Latino groups do not consider Latin America "as a distinct region to which they are particularly attached" (de la Garza et al. 1997, 413).

Overall, however, what is most notable about Latino involvement in foreign policy is how limited it has been. As Peter Hakim and Carlos Rosales point out in chapter 8, Latino leaders have played a very small role in major foreign policy initiatives and debates, including those affecting Latin America. Officials in the Clinton administration, for example, report that efforts to involve Latinos in the early planning of the Miami and Santiago Summits of the Americas proved fruitless. Although Latino leaders ultimately did participate in both meetings, they did so only at the last minute and in an ad hoc manner, and thus had less of an impact that they might have had.

Latinos are, however, attempting to engage in foreign policy issues more systematically. The first indicator of this was the creation in the 1980s of the Hispanic Council on Foreign Affairs (HCFA). HCFA was succeeded by the Hispanic Council on International Relations (HCIR), which was formally established in 1995. HCIR has 150 members and is funded by membership dues, foundation grants, and government contracts. Its mission is twofold: it seeks to educate Latinos about the local impact of global issues and to involve them in major foreign policy issues; it also seeks to promote Hispanics as experts on certain types of foreign policy issues, especially those involving Latin America. Its activities emphasize sponsoring or cosponsoring seminars entitled, for example, "The Future of Mexico," "NAFTA: Five-Year Review of Its Impact on Midwestern Communities," and "What's Asia Got to Do with Us?"

Such efforts notwithstanding, Hispanics have focused their energies on civil rights issues and on improving their economic condition, and this is the main factor explaining their limited involvement with international issues. Moreover, these same concerns have also influenced how they approach foreign policy when they occupy themselves with it. For example, Hispanic chambers of commerce were among NAFTA's most ardent promoters because Mexican officials persuaded them that it would create widespread opportunities for Hispanic businesses (Fajardo 1995). Even though that promise was never realized, Latino businesses and chambers of commerce continue to promote business ties with Latin America on the grounds that their linguistic and cultural roots uniquely qualify them to benefit from closer economic ties to the region (see chapter 3).

Similarly, Latino leaders use the logic of civil rights claims to demand greater representation in the institutions that are responsible for making foreign policy. Latino leaders cite the small numbers of Latino career foreign service officers (FSOs) as the basis for demanding changes in how FSOs are recruited, tested, trained, and promoted. Additionally, they demand an increase in the number of Latinos appointed as ambassadors and to other senior foreign service positions. Latino FSOs work with the advocacy groups and the Hispanic Congressional Caucus (HCC) to increase their numbers, and they are particularly involved with marshaling support from the HCC for Hispanic ambassadorial appointments (personal interviews with Hispanic FSOs, 1997–1999). Thus, for the same reasons that Latinos demand appointments in governmental institutions dealing with domestic issues, they demand positions in foreign policy–making agencies.

Predictably, Hispanic advocates emphasize appointments dealing with Latin America. They believe that Latinos are especially well qualified to understand the region and represent the nation in this hemisphere and to help the United States formulate policies that advance American interests while respecting regional sensitivities. This claim is supported by the extent to which Latinos report they are engaged with Latin America relative to other parts of the world (see chapter 2).

Hispanic FSOs, the only group of Latinos professionally engaged in foreign policy, partially agree with the arguments advanced by Latino advocates. A survey conducted by the Tomás Rivera Policy Institute as part of this project found that a majority of Latino FSOs agreed that their ethnicity made them more effective when they were stationed in Latin America.[8] Nonetheless, they do not emphasize Latin American appointments to the same extent as do Latino advocacy organizations. To the contrary, they recognize that successful careers require postings to a wide range of positions in geographically diverse regions. Indeed, until recently, repeated assignments to the *cucaracha circuit*, as Latin American posts are labeled, have signaled a failed career. While this may decline with the ascendancy of Mexico and the Southern Cone countries, for the foreseeable future, successful Hispanic FSOs, like all FSOs, will need experience beyond the region.

To an extent unappreciated by advocacy groups, therefore, Latino FSOs face major cross-pressures. On the one hand, because of their linguistic and cultural expertise, they may be pressured by senior department officials to accept assignments within the region. This, however, could lead to professional segregation, which damages career options. On the other hand, if they insist on postings outside the region, they neutralize the advantages their cultural and linguistic skills afford them and may alienate their superiors.

Whichever path they follow, many Hispanic FSOs must confront additional major obstacles. First, foreign officials are not always receptive to them. Ironically, this is at least as likely to occur in Latin America as in other parts of the world to which they are posted. Officials outside of Latin America sometimes do not understand that Hispanics are American, as is illustrated by a European official's asking a senior U.S.-born and -educated Hispanic FSO how he learned English so well.

Hispanic FSOs encounter two additional problems when they are assigned to Latin America. First, more than one-third reported that Anglo FSOs had *sometimes* or *often* accused them of having divided loyalties, that is, of placing the interests of the home country[9] on a par with or above U.S. interests. Second, Latin American governments have historically not welcomed Latino political appointees as ambassadors. Early in the Carter administration, for example, Colombia and Mexico made it clear that they would not accept Latino ambassadors. One likely reason for this was that "Mexicans want a true American and they know well the subordinate role that many Chicanos have played in the political and social affairs of the United States. . . . Mexicans must be dealing with people that have the right connections. . . . Mexicans unfortunately want an Anglo Ambassador" (del Castillo 1982). In other words, if Mexico and Colombia were to host political appointees, both governments would want them to be nationally influential. No Latino had that status in the 1970s. Additionally, Mexican objections reflected historically rooted prejudices against Mexican Americans (de la Garza 1980), a prejudice that also negatively affected how Mexican officials dealt with Julián Nava when Mexico finally agreed to accept an ambassador of Mexican American origin. Finally, Mexico, and perhaps other Latin American countries as well, are suspicious of Latino ambassadors because they see them as a Trojan horse. Senior members of the Secretaría de Relaciones Exteriores (SRE, Mexico's State Department) were critical of Nava's appointment for this reason (as reported in a personal interview with an SRE senior official). As Latinos have increased in stature, it seems clear that such attitudes have diminished.

Latino Participation in Foreign Policy

This, then, is the context within which Latinos are engaging in U.S. foreign policy in general and U.S.–Latin American relations in particular. Does this involvement undermine U.S. national interest, as Brimelow, Schlesinger, and Huntington argue? Does it support the national interest as traditionally defined? Do Latinos call for rearranging foreign policy priorities in the name of the national interest, just as interest groups have done historically? To answer these and other questions (such as how Latinos view these issues, the extent to which they are engaged in these processes, and the impact of their participation), the Tomás Rivera Policy Institute (TRPI) conducted four research projects, the results of which are reported in this volume. In addition to the survey of Hispanic FSOs mentioned previously, these include (1) a survey of Latino elites; (2) interviews with Latino community leaders, U.S. diplomatic officials in Latin America, Latin American diplomatic officials in the United States, and governmental and civic leaders in Latin America; and (3) evaluations of the results of these two studies by senior diplomatic officials from the four of the five countries on which the study focused—Mexico, the Dominican Republic, El Salvador, and Colombia[10]—and by Peter Romero, assistant secretary of State for Latin America; Peter Hakim and Carlos Rosales of the Inter American Dialogue; the nation's most prestigious nongovernmental organizations involved with Latin America; and Jorge Domínguez, a distinguished expert on U.S.–Latin American relations.

Overall, the results reveal several key patterns that merit discussion. The survey of Latin American elites (chapter 2) indicates that although, overall, Latino priorities are quite similar to those of Anglo elites, they also differ in meaningful ways. Most significantly, Latinos voice much weaker commitment to traditional defense policy and military alliances, and they are much more focused on Latin America than on Europe and other traditionally important regions. Surprisingly, they also are quite supportive of multilateral responses to crisis situations within specific countries, and they also voice greater support for unilateral U.S. responses to such developments than might be expected, especially with regard to Mexico. On the other hand, Latinos are ambivalent about the benefit of ethnic involvement in foreign policy. Nonetheless, approximately 25 percent say that ethnic NGOs should pursue their own policies, regardless of official U.S. policies.

Those concerned about Latinos undermining the national interest may well point to this last result to support their case. We would note, however, that other groups have not been asked similar questions, so there is no basis for comparing Latinos to other groups on this dimension. We know, though, that oil companies have continued to trade with their Middle Eastern partners, even after such trade was prohibited. Similarly, numerous cities openly challenged U.S. policy in Central America by declaring themselves refugee centers. Finally, Col. Oliver North's support for the Contras indicates that even governmental actors pursue specific goals that are counter to official policy. In other words, Latino attitudes toward autonomous foreign policy behavior that is counter to official policy may be more the norm than the exception. Moreover, the wide range of actors who, whether they are motivated by pure self-interest or by the belief that their activities actually serve the national interest, engage in activities contrary to official policy, suggests the utility of conceptualizing the national interest as a political concept rather than one that is above politics. In other words, groups seem more willing to adhere to policies that support their interests than to policies that harm them, even if those policies serve the greater good. Regardless of whether or not one agrees with this focus, it is far from the anti-American agenda that, according to Brimelow, Schlesinger, and Huntington, Latinos advocate.

The extent to which Latinos are involved in international relations and foreign policy is described in chapter 3. Additionally, the chapter reviews how emigrants are viewed by the governments and societies of their countries of origin. This is the first empirical assessment of the interactions between Latinos and their historical homelands.

It is noteworthy that the representatives of the several embassies who commented on the study endorsed its major conclusions (chapters 4–7). Everyone agreed, for example, that narco-traffic, immigration, and remittances were the key issues in U.S.–Latin American relations. Not all of the issues are relevant in all cases, however. Thus, while drugs are key in U.S.–Colombian relations, migration and remittances are not. In El Salvador, on the other hand, drugs are much less significant than migration and remittances.

Perhaps the most interesting criticism of the findings came from Mexico. Gustavo Mohar suggests that the study overemphasizes the significance of remittances. He supports his argument by pointing out that the contribution that remittances make to national accounts is declining; moreover, remittances are concentrated in one hundred communities and therefore cannot be nationally significant. This argument ignores the continued growth in the absolute value of remittances, which now is estimated at $6 billion annually. Also, Mohar's response diminishes the extent to which the "one hundred communities" depend on these moneys. More significantly, his argument ignores these communities' concentration within specific states; consequently, the cumulative impact of these sums on states such as Guanajuato is far greater than he acknowledges. Indeed, there is little doubt that these states would experience either massive migration or significant political instability that would have national repercussions if remittances were terminated. Mohar's unwillingness or inability to acknowledge the significance of these sums may be an example of Mexico's deeply rooted disdain for emigrants. Whatever drives this view, it is especially ironic that it is being voiced at the same time that the Mexican government has institutionalized programs intended to strengthen the relationship between emigrants and Mexico.

Another significant finding is that there is no consensus regarding the development of ethnic lobbies. Bernando Vega, the Dominican ambassador, clearly advocates developing such a lobby, and he believes it is already becoming effective. Ambassador Fernando Cepeda Ulloa is extremely dubious that Colombians can achieve this, and Gustavo Mohar offers a sober assessment of the limits of such a relationship. Furthermore, Secretary Peter Romero (chapter 9) does not foresee the establishment of country-specific ethnic lobbies that would pit the interests of specific countries against U.S. interest, initiatives that would surely trouble him. Instead, he expects and is very supportive of the prospect that Latinos will increasingly engage in Latin American issues in ways that will further U.S. policies throughout the region.

The final pattern we will comment on here is the difference between Latino involvement with Latin America around cultural, economic, and social issues, and how disengaged Latinos are from foreign policy issues. As chapter 2 documents, Latinos regularly travel to Latin America, and they do a considerable amount of business throughout the region. As Hakim and Rosales note (chapter 8), however, they do not engage in the foreign policy process per se. While there is no doubt that the need to protect familial and business relationships may lead to mobilizing Latinos around foreign policy issues, such as occurred in response to the government's efforts to repatriate undocumented Salvadoran immigrants following the end of the civil war, Latinos do not engage in the regular foreign policy process. When they do, as was evident in the NAFTA negotiations, they argue in defense of their domestic concerns and not on behalf of foreign interests. In sum, as Jorge Domínguez notes in his conclusion (chapter 10), their foreign policy behavior explicitly contradicts the indictments voiced by Huntington et al.

Overall, the study offers two conclusions: (1) Latinos are not actively involved in foreign policy, and; (2) there is no clear pattern that defines the relationship between emigrants and their countries of origin. Domínguez's chapter suggests a variety of explanations to account for these results, and he also evaluates the likely practical impact of these findings for U.S.–Latin American relations. His insights clearly reject the arguments of those who overstate Latino involvement so as to celebrate its significance, as well as those of people who exaggerate it and consequently fuel anti-Latino discrimination and make the nation feel threatened.

This volume, then, should be seen as the first systematic effort to establish an empirical baseline against which future Latino foreign policy activities may be compared. We hope the work presented here will stimulate research with regard to both the level and the type of Latino foreign policy activities. We also hope that it will contribute to sober rather than inflamed debate regarding the contributions that Latinos will make to foreign policy and to the continuous evolution of the meaning of the "national interest."

Notes

1. "Latino" and "Hispanic" are used interchangeably to refer to individuals who can trace their ancestry to Spanish-speaking countries in the Western Hemisphere.

2. It is noteworthy that he cites no evidence that bilingual Hispanics are less supportive of American values than are English monolinguals.

3. Schlesinger seems to confuse support for bilingualism, which means fluency in two languages, for instance, English and Spanish, with support for monolingualism, for instance, fluency only in Spanish. Latino elites are strongly supportive of the former and reject the latter.

4. Ronald Steel echoed these views with regard to a similar effort by the Pacific Council on International Policy. See "Who Is Us?" *The New Republic*, September 14-21, 1998, 13.

5. The only noteworthy exception to this pattern has been the Puerto Rican Independence Movement. Its spectacular attacks on the House of Representatives and other, lessnotorious, terrorist incidents notwithstanding, its impact on national stability has been negligible.

6. *Hispanos* is the label which New Mexico's Spanish-origin population has used to identify itself.

7. Although the available data on Cuban Americans and Puerto Ricans does not permit the same level of analysis, these same patterns also appear to characterize both groups.

8. Those responding to the survey do not constitute a representative sample. There-fore, these responses should be viewed as insights into the Latino FSO experience rather than as statistically reliable data.

9. The home country, or the country to which they were posted?

10. Guatemalan officials did not submit a formal response to the study. However, the Honorable Alfonso Quiñones, Guatemala's Ambassador to the Organization of American States, was present at the seminar on June 25, 1998, where the report was reviewed, and at that time he expressed his agreement with its findings.

References

Acuña, Rodolfo. 1988. *Occupied America: A History of Chicanos*. 3rd ed. New York: Harper & Row.

Ahrari, Mohammed E., ed. 1987. *Ethnic Groups and U.S. Foreign Policy*. Westport, Conn.: Greenwood Press.

Alterman, Eric. 1998. *Who Speaks for America? Why Democracy Matters in Foreign Policy*. Ithaca, N.Y.: Cornell University Press.

Brimelow, Peter. 1996. *Alien Nation*. New York: Harper Perennial.

DeConde, Alexander. 1992. *Ethnicity, Race and American Foreign Policy*. Boston: North-eastern University Press.

de la Garza, Rodolfo O. 1980. "Chicanos and U.S. Foreign Policy: The Future of Chicano-Mexican Relations." *Western Political Science Quarterly* 33, no. 4 (December): 571–82.

de la Garza, Rodolfo O., F. Chris García, and Angelo Falcón. 1996. "Will the Real Ameri-cans Please Stand Up? Mexican American and Anglo Support for Core American Values." *American Journal of Political Science* 40 (May): 335–51.

de la Garza, Rodolfo O., and Louis DeSipio. 1998. "Interests Not Passions: Mexican American Attitudes toward Mexico and Issues Shaping U.S.–Mexico Relations." *International Migration Review* 32 (summer): 401–22.

de la Garza, Rodolfo O., J. Hernández, A. Falcón, F. Chris García, and J. García. 1997. "Mexican, Puerto Rican and Cuban Foreign Policy Perspectives." In F. Chris García, ed., *Pursuing Power: Latinos and the Political System*. Notre Dame, Ind.: University of Notre Dame Press, 401–25.

del Castillo, Gustavo. Personal interview, San Diego, Calif., June 27, 1982.

Eisenstadt, Todd. 1997. "The Rise of the Mexican Lobby in Washington: Even Further from God and Even Closer to the United States?" In Rodolfo O. de la Garza and Jesús Velasco, eds., *Bridging the Border: Transforming Mexico–U.S. Relations*. Boul-der, Colo.: Rowman & Littlefield, pp.: 89–124.

Fajardo, Richard. 1995. *Latino Businesses and NAFTA in Southern California*. Claremont, Calif.: Tomás Rivera Center.

Fuchs, Lawrence H. 1990. *The American Kaleidoscope: Race, Ethnicity, and the Civic Culture*. Hanover, N.H.: University Press of New England.

Huntington, Samuel P. 1991. *American Politics: The Politics of Disharmony*. Cambridge, Mass.: Belknap Press of Harvard University Press.

———. 1996. *The Clash of Civilizations and the Remaking of World Order.* New York: Simon & Schuster.

———. 1997. "The Erosion of American National Interests." *Foreign Affairs* (September/October): 28–49.

Otero, Miguel Antonio. 1940. *My Nine Years As Governor of the Territory of New Mexico, 1897–1906.* Albuquerque: University of New Mexico Press.

Schlesinger, Arthur M., Jr. 1992. *The Disuniting of America: Reflections on a Multicultural Society.* New York: Norton.

Smith, Tom. 1990. "Ethnic Survey." GSS Topical Report No. 19. Chicago: National Opinion Research Center, University of Chicago.

Stevens, Gillian. 1994. "Immigrants, Emigration, Language Acquisition, and the English Language Proficiency of Immigrants in the U.S." In Barry Edmonston and Jeffrey S. Passel, eds., *Immigration and Ethnicity: The Integration of America's Newest Arrivals.* Washington, D.C.: Urban Institute Press, 163–85.

Tomás Rivera Center. 1995. *Latinos in Texas: A Socio-Demographic Profile.* Claremont, Calif.

Trubowitz, Peter. 1997. *Defining the National Interest: Conflict and Change in American Foreign Policy.* Chicago: University of Chicago Press.

U.S. Immigration and Naturalization Service. 1999. *1997 Statistical Yearbook of the Immigration and Naturalization Service.* Springfield, Va.: National Technical Information Service.

PART II

LATINOS AND FOREIGN POLICYMAKING

2
Foreign Policy Perspectives of Hispanic Elites

Harry P. Pachon and Rodolfo O. de la Garza with Adrián D. Pantoja

S cholars have begun to display much more interest in studying the Hispanic diaspora and its possible transnational links with Latin America. As the previous chapter discusses, the growing U.S.–Hispanic population; the relatively recent diasporas of large communities of Mexicans, Cubans, Dominicans, Salvadorans, Colombians, and Nicaraguans into the mainland United States; and the North American Free Trade Agreement induced economic integration of the North American economy have raised concerns about how Latinos view U.S.–Latin American relations. Will these Hispanic subgroups identify with their homelands in a way that is inimical to U.S. interests? Do Latino communities and their leaders resonate to mainstream American foreign policy goals? How do Latinos rank U.S. foreign policy concerns vis-à-vis domestic policy concerns? These are questions that have been the subject of general speculation (Huntington

1997, Schlesinger 1991), but, aside from anecdotal accounts, few works have systematically analyzed Hispanic attitudes and perceptions regarding U.S.–Latin American relations (de la Garza 1987, Fernández 1987). This chapter is an attempt to fill this void by analyzing the results of a national survey of 454 Hispanic leaders carried out by Public Agenda and the Tomás Rivera Policy Institute (TRPI) in the fall and winter of 1997 (Public Agenda and Tomás Rivera Policy Institute 1998). The sampling frame for this study was generated by researchers at TRPI under the direction of the authors from lists and directories of influential Latino community members, Hispanic elected officials, civic and corporate leaders, and heads of nongovernmental organizations (NGOs) at the national and local levels. Respondents fell into six categories: nonprofit directors (15%), media representatives (20%), public officials (13%), business leaders (21%), academics (27%), and influential persons from other fields (12%).·

Letters describing the purpose of the survey and requesting their involvement were mailed to this database of approximately 4,000 Hispanic leaders. Approximately 509 agreed to participate. The survey was mailed to these respondents and to an additional 871 respondents from a Public Agenda database of Hispanic leaders. Thirty-three percent ($n = 459$) of these individuals responded to the mail questionnaire. Public Agenda conducted additional telephone interviews to gain more insight into the responses. While the results from this survey do not constitute a true random sample of Latino leaders, the results may suggest general trends and tendencies for the group in general and indicate possible interesting subgroup differences.

We will first explore the overall rankings of Hispanic leaders' foreign policy concerns versus domestic policy issues. We then will compare how Hispanic leaders and U.S. leaders in general rank foreign policy issues and the emphasis each group places on Latin America. Finally, we will explore differences among Hispanic subgroups.

The Salience of
Domestic Policy Concerns for Hispanic Leaders

A priori, two equally plausible theories can be argued to explain the relative importance of domestic versus foreign policy goals for Latino leaders. One perspective would hold that, since the Latino community has a high proportion of foreign-born, first-generation immigrants, Latino leaders will give greater importance to U.S. foreign policy issues in general, specifically, those that affect Latin America, since U.S. foreign policy actions have an impact on Latinos' historical homelands.

An alternative perspective would be that Latino leaders, composed of both native-and foreign-born individuals, will place greater importance on domestic policy issues, since these policies are the ones that most directly affect Hispanic communities in the States. To determine the relative saliency of both sets of issues, the TRPI/Public Agenda survey asked Hispanic leaders to rank the importance of eighteen public policy issues; twelve of the eighteen were foreign policy issues.

As table 2.1 indicates, Hispanic leaders overwhelmingly place domestic policy issues among the top five policy goals the United States should have. Nine out of ten Latino leaders rank education as a "very important" policy goal. Closely following education are the domestic issues of "improving race and ethnic relations," "maintaining economic growth," and "reducing crime." The saliency and importance of U.S. domestic policy issues for Latino leaders is further evidenced by the finding that five of the six domestic policy issues on the list are considered "very important" by over half of the Latino leaders. As table 2.1 indicates, only "preventing the spread of nuclear weapons" is ranked as one of the top five issues by these Latino leaders.

The saliency of domestic policy issues to Latino leaders is further substantiated by the fact that nearly 87 percent of them say U.S. Latinos should be most concerned with the well-being of the Latino community in the United States. Another three out of four Latino leaders also say that "what happens to the Hispanic/Latino community in the United States is more important to me than the state of U.S. relations with Latin America." "We should cultivate our own garden," said one survey respondent in a follow-up interview. "We should be focused on the amelioration of conditions here in the United States," said another.

Leaders born in the United States are more likely to focus on the U.S.–Hispanic community than on Latin America (81%). Yet even two out of three Latino leaders born in Latin America (64%) concur with the perspective of placing priority on domestic issues rather than on foreign policy concerns.

Despite these concerns with domestic policy issues, Hispanic leaders have hardly turned their backs on Latin America; in fact, as individuals they have a wide web of relations and points of contact with the region and routinely track what goes on there. Almost nine out of ten Hispanic leaders (87%) report they closely follow current events in Latin America. Almost all (92%) have been to Latin America, and more than half of these (59%) have traveled there within the last twelve months.

What is more, their social contacts, friends, family, and colleagues reinforce and remind them of their connection to Latin America. More than half (52%) have participated in activities regarding U.S.–Latin American affairs that range from writing letters to offering expert advice to participating in associations. Almost three-quarters (74%) say that at least some of their Latino colleagues at work or their friends keep close track of events in Latin America, and 40 percent work for organizations that have extensive dealings in Latin America. Two-thirds have relatives in Latin America, and of these, 66 percent maintain regular contact with them. It is perhaps not surprising to note that leaders born in Latin America

Table 2.1: Importance of U.S. Policy Goals by Latino Leaders

Here is a list of possible policy goals that the U.S. might have. For each, please mark whether you think that it should be:	Very important (%)	Somewhat important (%)	Not at all important (%)	Don't know (%)
Improving education	95	5	*	*
Improving race and ethnic relations	80	19	1	*
Maintaining economic growth	76	23	1	–
Preventing the spread of nuclear weapons	62	32	5	1
Reducing crime	61	36	3	1
Improving the U.S. environment	60	38	1	–
Stopping the flow of illegal drugs into the U.S.	54	36	9	1
Improving the global environment	46	49	3	2
Combating world hunger	41	53	5	2
Combating international terrorism	40	48	10	2
Improving U.S. relations with other nations	40	55	4	1
Protecting the jobs of American workers	39	48	12	1
Promoting and defending human rights in other countries	35	55	9	1
Reducing our trade deficit with foreign countries	21	60	16	3
Maintaining superior military power worldwide	20	49	27	3
Strengthening the United Nations	19	53	25	4
Controlling & reducing illegal/ undocumented immigration	14	51	34	2
Defending our allies' security	8	60	29	4

Note: Results of less than 1% are signified by "*"; no response is signified by "–."
Source: Public Agenda and Tomás Rivera Policy Institute, *Here to Stay: The Domestic and International Priorities of Latino Leaders*, New York and Claremont, Calif., 1998.

are more likely to follow events in the region very closely than are those born in the United States (54% compared with 30%), to have relatives in Latin America (84% to 56%), and to stay in close touch with those relatives (82% to 51% among those with relatives). In the end—whether through personal ties or professional action or both—the relationship between Hispanic leaders and Latin America is a close one.

Comparing the General Foreign Policy Concerns of Latino and U.S. Leaders

Although Hispanic leaders are fundamentally concerned with domestic matters and the well-being of the U.S.–Hispanic community, they are hardly isolationists, as they share with other U.S. leaders surveyed in the past a global perspective and a proclivity toward an activist U.S. foreign policy. About nine in ten (89%) think it is better for the future of the United States to take an active part in world affairs than to stay out. Only 11 percent of Latino leaders responding to this survey say "keeping involvement abroad to a minimum" should be a top priority for U.S. foreign policy. In Public Agenda's 1995 study of the foreign policy views of a broad sample of U.S. leaders, 14 percent responded the same way. In a separate Gallup survey of the foreign policy views of a broad sample of American leaders, 98 percent wanted the United States to take an active part in world affairs, as did 65 percent of the general public.

Latino Leaders' Focus on Latin America

Hispanic leaders want the United States to adopt an activist foreign policy not only on the world scene but in Latin American as well. Eighty-five percent say the United States should be paying more attention to its relations with Latin America. Hispanic leaders are convinced greater U.S. activity will have positive consequences for Latin America. Seven in ten (71%) say that more U.S. activity in the region would be better for Latin America. "I think on the whole the U.S.– Latin American relationship has been beneficial," said one respondent. To say the United States should maintain—and even enhance—its engagement in Latin American affairs is one thing, but toward which goals?

Two Pillars: Trade and Democracy

Hispanic leaders want two policy themes to drive U.S. objectives in Latin America: improvement in trade and development, and strengthening of democracy and human rights. More than half (56%) of Latino leaders give top priority to the U.S. increasing trade, economic growth, and development in its relations with Latin America. Asked to choose the one issue that deserves the highest priority from a list of seven including limiting political instability, controlling drug trafficking, and protecting the environment, a plurality (44%) opt for trade and growth.

The focus on economic relations plays out in concrete terms: the North American Free Trade Agreement (NAFTA) is extremely popular among Hispanic leaders as a good pattern to replicate in U.S.–Latin American trade relations. Seven in ten (69%) say the United States should use the NAFTA model to extend free trade with other Latin American countries. What is more, although support for the extension of NAFTA is, not surprisingly, greatest among the business leaders surveyed (81%), the sentiment is shared by respondents working in the nonprofit, academic, media, and political sectors as well. Finally, 77 percent of Hispanic leaders think the future holds greater interdependence between U.S. and Latin American economies.

But Hispanic leaders do not want U.S.–Latin American relations to be only about business: a little more than half (52%) also want support for democracy and human rights to be a central pillar of policy toward the region. This is a democratic hemisphere, stated one leader, "so we need fair elections and rule of law."

Some believe that democracy and economic growth are so intertwined that one trend will reinforce the other and that both must therefore be pursued simultaneously. "[The United States] should favor pluralistic democracies and the liberalization of markets with less governmental control," said a Hispanic leader. I think there's a very firm link between economic liberalism and limited constitutional governments. You can't have one without the other. Another leader echoed this feeling: Just as happened in Europe with the collapse of authoritarian regimes, it's clear that a free economy and democracy go hand in hand.

There is also a sense that Hispanic leaders should try to move the United States toward tying regional trade to support for human rights. Fully 75 percent of Hispanic leaders surveyed say U.S. Latinos should push for linking trade and aid to advances in democracy and human rights in Latin America. "But there are limits," counseled one leader. "We shouldn't link trade completely to how pure the democracy is or how pure the economy is."

The Role of Drugs
in U.S.–Latin American Relations

Are the priorities of U.S. Latinos in line with current U.S. policy toward the region? Latino leaders do not think so. More than four in ten (44%) say that if they had to choose one issue that deserves highest priority in U.S.–Latin American relations, they would choose increasing trade, economic growth, and development. But only 22 percent believe that this is what gets highest priority from the United States. And while another 28 percent would choose support for democracy and for human rights as their top priority, only 4 percent believe that this is currently what the United States focuses on.

Instead, the perception among the plurality of Hispanic leaders (41%) is that the predominant U.S. objective in Latin America is combating drug trafficking. And while this objective is important in the eyes of Hispanics, many also believe it overwhelms and obscures other important aspects of relations with Latin America. One leader said, "To a certain extent, the drug problem does overshadow our relations with some countries." Another commented, "We shouldn't stop trying to deal with the drug crisis, but there's more to life than drugs. There's a need for U.S. involvement in the region that has nothing to do with drugs."

Latino leaders would also place less emphasis on illegal immigration. While only 12 percent believe the issue should be a top priority, 25 percent say it currently gets the most attention from the United States.

Hispanic Leaders' Perceptions Compared with Those of the American Public

Some interesting differences come to light when Hispanic leaders' priorities are compared with those of the U.S. public in general. The general public seems to place a good deal more importance on stopping both illegal immigration and drugs than do Hispanic leaders. In a 1995 Gallup poll, 72 percent of the public said controlling and reducing illegal immigration should be a top priority; in a 1997 Pew study, 42 percent said reducing illegal immigration should be a top priority. But only 14 percent of the Latino leaders said it was very important to reduce illegal immigration.

Whereas the illegal drug issue troubles Latino leaders, the general public seems even more concerned. In the Gallup poll, 85 percent of the public said that controlling the flow of illegal drugs should be a top priority for the United States; in the Pew poll, 67 percent responded in this way. But 54 percent of Latino leaders responding to our survey said stopping the flow of illegal drugs should be a very important policy goal. In follow-up interviews, several suggested that immigration and illegal drugs were top public concerns because of media coverage: "That's what the public hears, because that's what the press tells them. But that doesn't mean that's all the public wants; they just don't know."

Although the views of Hispanic leaders may differ from the public's, as table 2.2 shows, they are not so different from those of U.S. leaders overall. While 72 percent of the public wants curbing illegal immigration to be a top priority, only 21

Table 2.2: Hispanic and U.S. Leaders Foreign Policy Goals

Issue	% U.S. leaders saying issue is "very important"	% Latino leaders saying issue is "very important"	Rank of issue to U.S. leaders	Rank of issue to Hispanic leaders
Preventing spread of nuclear weapons	90	62	1	1
Defending allies' security	60	8	2	8
Stopping illegal drugs	57	54	3	3
Maintaining superior military power	54	20	4	9
Protecting U.S. jobs	50	39	5	5
Improving the global environment	49	60	6	2
Combating world hunger	41	41	7	4
Reducing trade deficit	49	21	8	6
Reducing illegal immigration	28	14	9	7

Source: U.S. leaders: John E. Rielley, American Public Opinion and U.S. Foreign Policy 1995, Chicago: Chicago Council on Foreign Relations. Hispanic leaders: Public Agenda and Tomás Rivera Policy Institute, *Here to Stay: The Domestic and International Priorities of Latino Leaders*, New York and Claremont, Calif., 1998.

percent of a broad sample of American leaders surveyed by Gallup says that this is a very important goal for the United States (compared to 14% of Hispanic leaders). While 85 percent of the public thinks controlling drugs is a very important goal, only 57 percent of U.S. leaders agree (as do 54% of Hispanic leaders). Thus the decreased emphasis Latino leaders place on these issues may be more a function of their status as leaders than of their being Hispanic.

Latino Leaders' Connection to Latin America

The strong connection that Latino leaders have to Latin America—to Mexico especially—parallels their desire to put that area front and center in U.S. policy.

When asked to rank eleven countries and regions in order of importance to the
United States, more than half of Hispanic leaders (57%) placed Mexico either
first or second. By contrast, only half as many (28%) gave Western Europe the
same ranking. Other regions that have traditionally garnered substantial attention in U.S. policy were seen as top-ranking by even smaller percentages: Only
about one-fifth of Hispanic leaders (23%) ranked Asia, the Middle East (22%),
and Canada (21%) first or second.

In follow-up interviews, leaders talked about the proximity of Mexico, its
trade with the United States, and the crossover in population to explain why they
thought Mexico was so important. "Mexico is the great Hispanic neighbor, the
one that has the most clout," said one leader. "We have more investment in it than
any other Hispanic country in the area—even before NAFTA." But there seemed
to be another reason as well, a sense that there is an imbalance in U.S. foreign
policy, an inattentiveness toward Latin America in general and toward Mexico
especially that needs to be redressed. "Mexico is very important, it needs to be
higher on America's priority list," one said. Another leader said: "I don't know
what our policy is. . . . I'm not even sure we have a concerted policy effort toward Latin America."

Most leaders interviewed after the survey did not think the issue was a zero-
sum game; they were not calling for attenuation of U.S. relations with Europe or
Asia, but simply saw a need to pay increased attention to Latin America. "Japan
and China are the future, and Europe, too, not just because of the past but for
economic and other reasons," said one respondent, "so it doesn't make sense to
change our focus, but it makes tremendous sense to enlarge our focus to include
Latin America." Another said, "Some reorientation toward South America is necessary, but I don't view it as a zero-sum game regarding attention to Europe."

One leader saw the issue in blunter realpolitik terms: "Is there a huge army
in Latin America? Are there atom bombs? China has a huge population and the
atom bomb. No country in Latin America competes with that. So our focus is a
matter of practicality." But even he thought inadequate attention was being paid
to Latin America.

Ethnic versus National Interests

Hispanic leaders, however, do not believe that the involvement of ethnic groups
in U.S. foreign policy has always worked to the benefit of the United States and,
perhaps for that reason, prefer a moderate approach to their own involvement.
When Hispanic leaders were asked to assess the impact of such ethnic groups as
the Irish, the Jews, or the Cubans on U.S. foreign policy, 20 percent believed that
those groups had tended to harm the U.S. national interest; 13 percent said they

had benefited the national interest. The majority (54%) said that these groups have had mixed effects. One interviewee expressed misgivings about the Cuban lobby and cited it as an example of what not to do: "It's a group that concentrates all their energies on one issue. . . . This one group has held U.S. policy toward Cuba hostage, and I don't think that should be the goal."

Most Hispanic leaders believe they have an obligation to work within the framework and bounds of official U.S. foreign policy. Forced to choose among three roles Hispanic organizations could play from working independently regardless of U.S. policy, to working on behalf of U.S. policy, to working independently but not in contravention of U.S. policy most Hispanic leaders choose the moderate course. Only one-fourth (26%) say U.S.–Latino organizations should pursue their own objectives regardless of U.S. policy, another fourth (24%) believe the opposite, that they are obligated to coordinate action with the government in support of U.S. goals in Latin America. The plurality (43%) believes it appropriate to pursue their own objectives independently in Latin America as long as they do not contravene U.S. foreign policy priorities or interests. "We should influence it [foreign policy toward Latin America] but not monopolize it," said one leader. "At the end of the day we are just part of this greater community of the United States. Just because we know it better doesn't mean we have the right answers."

The Foreign Policy Goals of Latino and U.S. Leaders

If one compares the foreign policy issues ranked by Latino leaders in table 2.1 to the goals U.S. leaders in general named in the Chicago Council on Foreign Relations 1995 report[1] the following major differences emerge. Latinos rank the environment and world hunger as much more significant than maintaining military power and defending allies' security. What are the implications of these findings? Combining the fact that Latino leaders give first priority to domestic issues with these foreign policy priorities may mean that they may begin pushing the nation away from traditional foreign policy concerns toward international priorities that have more immediately linked to domestic issues.

What explains these distinctive patterns? Perhaps it is the lack of historical involvement in the foreign policy process and with organizations such as the Council on Foreign Relations, which provide members in-depth exposure to the paradigms that govern U.S. foreign policy objectives. It may also be that Latinos bring a distinctive perspective to foreign policy, one that combines their experiences as Americans with their understanding of Latin America. In other words, just as gender (Togeby 1994) and religion (Jelen 1994) affect foreign policy preferences, the ethnic experience may shape how Latinos view international issues.

Hispanic Subgroup Differences

The differences in the history and socioeconomic standings of the major subgroups constituting the U.S.–Hispanic population, that is, Mexican Americans, Puerto Ricans, Cuban Americans, and others, may conceal important subgroup variations in any discussion of Latinos in general. Disaggregating our survey responses and comparing the variations among Mexican Americans, Cuban Americans, and Puerto Ricans, as well as those between native- and foreign-born Hispanics, yield interesting differences. As table 2.3 indicates, domestic policy issues for all three Latino subgroups clearly rank higher than foreign policy issues among Hispanic leaders in general. Education (94.5%), improving race relations (79.5%), maintaining economic growth (75.3%), and reducing crime (60.4%) score higher than most foreign policy issues among Hispanic leaders in general. Differences do emerge across nationalities, however. For example, maintaining economic growth scored differently among Mexican Americans (72.5%) than among Cuban

Table 2.3: Hispanic Leaders Ranking of Foreign Versus Domestic Policy Priorities for the United States

	Hispanic leaders	Mexican American	Cuban American	Puerto Rican	Native born	Foreign born
Education	94.5%	95.8%	92.2%	95.8%	94.2%	94.9%
Improving race and ethnic relations	79.5%	83.1%	68.6%	87.5%	80.4%	78.1%
Maintaining economic growth	75.3%	72.5%	92.2%	62.5%	72.7%	79.2%
Reducing crime	60.4%	56.6%	60.8%	50.0%	56.4%	66.9%
Improving the U.S. environment	59.9%	59.8%	64.7%	54.2%	57.8%	63.5%
Combating international terrorism	40.1%	34.9%	66.7%	29.2%	36.0%	46.1%
Improving U.S. relations with other nations	39.6%	33.9%	52.9%	39.6%	35.3%	46.1%
Strengthening the United States	18.7%	13.8%	13.7%	18.8%	16.7%	21.9%

Source: Public Agenda and Tomás Rivera Policy Institute, New York and Claremont, Calif., 1998.

Table 2.4: Hispanic Leaders Ranking of Long-Range U.S. Foreign Policy Goals: Percent Saying "Top Priority"

	Hispanic leaders	Mexican American	Cuban American	Puerto Rican	Native born	Foreign born
Pursuing international trade and business opportunities	55%	50.8%	60.8%	62.5%	55.3%	52.8%
Protecting the global environment	53%	22.2%	58.8%	52.1%	30.9%	36.5%
Supporting democracy and human rights abroad	49%	43.4%	66.7%	52.1%	44.7%	55.1%
Limiting conflicts in areas important to the U.S.	34%	49.7%	54.9%	41.7%	52.0%	53.9%
Helping the economies of developing countries (U.S. leadership wording: "underdeveloped nations"	30%	29.6%	21.6%	29.2%	29.1%	30.9%
Keeping U.S. involvement to a minimum	14%	11.1%	11.8%	18.8%	12.4%	15.2%

Source: Public Agenda and Tomás Rivera Policy Institute, New York and Claremont, Calif., 1998.

Americans (92.2%). Puerto Ricans scored this issue (62.5%) closer to Mexican American leaders than to Cuban American leaders.

Differences are also detected with regard to combating international terrorism and improving U.S. relations with other nations. In both cases, Cuban American respondents show a greater interest in supporting these goals than do Mexican American and Puerto Rican respondents. Finally, slight differences are noted among native- and foreign-born respondents, although no clear pattern is detected, nor does any one issue appear to generate a significant difference.

In terms of long-range foreign policy goals (table 2.4), a different picture emerges when we disaggregate the responses. Two issues, democratization/human rights and the protection of the global environment, generate more widespread support among Cuban American than among Mexican American leaders. High Cuban American support for human rights and democratization is understandable, given that these issues have been central in Cuban American opposition to Fidel Castro's government.

Puerto Ricans, like Cuban Americans, display greater concern for international trade and the environment than do Mexican American leaders, although their concern for human rights and democratization parallels the Mexican American response rate. Cuban Americans' high level of support for international trade and business opportunities may also reflect the fact that many of the middle- and upper-class Cubans who fled Castro's regime were disproportionately engaged in international trade, sugar production, and tourism. It may also mirror the salience of entrepreneurship in the Cuban American community in South Florida.

No major differences were noted among Mexican Americans, Cuban Americans, Puerto Ricans, or native- and foreign-born Hispanics in regard to the role the United States should play in world affairs and Latin America in particular (table 2.5)

Among foreign-born Hispanics leaders, there is an interest (64%) in events and developments in Latin America (see table 2.6). When asked to rank thirteen Latin American countries in terms of how closely they follow issues there, more than half (54.8%) of Hispanic leaders in general placed Mexico either first or second; Cuba followed Mexico. Not surprisingly, the results also indicate that both Mexican Americans and Cuban Americans follow developments in their countries of origin more closely than those in any other country. Perhaps more surprisingly, Puerto Ricans also scored Mexico (35.4%) and Cuba (33.3%) higher than any other Latin American country. Because Puerto Rico was not listed among

Table 2.5: Latino Leaders Perceptions of U.S. Role in International Affairs

	Latino leaders	Mexican American	Cuban American	Puerto Rican	Foreign born	Native born
Active	98%	90%	85%	92%	85%	90%
Stay out	1%	7%	10%	8%	11%	8%
Don't know	1%	2%	2%	–	3%	2%

Source: Public Agenda and Tomás Rivera Policy Institute, New York and Claremont, Calif., 1998.

Table 2.6: Hispanic Leaders Interest in Latin America

	Total Hispanic leaders	Mexican American	Cuban American	Puerto Rican	Native born	Foreign born
More interested in Latin America	56.0%	57%	50%	51%	52%	64%
More interested in some other region	7%	9%	10%	10%	9%	5%
Interested in both the same	33%	32%	38%	37%	36%	29%
Don't know	1%	1%	0%	0%	1%	1%

Source: Public Agenda and Tomás Rivera Policy Institute, New York and Claremont, Calif., 1998.

the possible choices, however, the "other" category received a higher score (37.5%) than Mexico and Cuba from Puerto Ricans.

Foreign Policy Scenario Preferences

Hispanic leaders were asked about six foreign policy scenarios and possible U.S. responses. The options in each scenario can be classified into two major categories of policy tools: multilateral response diplomatic, economic, or military in conjunction with Latin American allies; or unilateral diplomatic, economic, or military without any assistance. In the first scenario, a crisis in Haiti (table 2.7), Hispanic leaders prefer multilateral diplomatic and economic responses in cooperation with Latin American allies. A greater percentage of Cuban American leaders than leaders from other Hispanic groups, however, indicate that they would be willing to support unilateral military intervention to meet such a crisis.

The second scenario involves the military overthrow of a democratically elected government, whereby the outgoing government requests U.S. assistance to restore democracy. Once again, Hispanic leaders show a greater willingness to pursue political or economic means in cooperation with other Latin American allies than to take unilateral action, and Cuban Americans show a greater willingness to undertake unilateral military intervention (table 2.8).

The third scenario involves a Latin American government engaging in systematic torture and violation of human rights. It should be recalled that Hispanic leaders in general, with higher support among Cuban Americans, show great interest in supporting democratization and the protection of human rights. Most favor the use of political and economic instruments to achieve policy objectives aimed at punishing those who violate civil and human rights. While Cuban Americans again demonstrate a greater propensity toward unilateral military intervention than do other groups, the level is not as high as in the previous two scenarios (table 2.9).

The fourth scenario, like the first, focuses on a specific country, Cuba. This scenario involves Fidel Castro's dying, the ensuing political and economic chaos, and the U.S. response. Again, Hispanic leaders in general favor diplomatic and economic response in collaboration with other Latin American governments, while a plurality of Cuban Americans favor unilateral military intervention (see table 2.10).

The final two scenarios focus on Mexico, the centerpiece for Hispanic leaders. In the first scenario, a drug kingpin is living openly in Mexico, flooding the

Table 2.7: Haiti Scenario

Suppose there are major economic and civil-political disturbances in Haiti that prompt a massive emigration to the U.S.

Should the U.S.:	Hispanic leaders	Mexican American	Cuban American	Puerto Rican	Native born	Foreign born
Stay out	6.8%	6.3%	3.9%	8.3%	8.4%	4.5%
Respond with diplomatic and economic means, but only in cooperation with other Latin American countries	39.0%	42.9%	15.7%	39.6%	36.7%	42.1%
Respond with diplomatic and economic means, even if alone	29.5%	33.9%	27.5%	27.1%	32.7%	24.7%
Respond with military means, but only in cooperation with other Latin American countries	10.1%	5.8%	17.6%	18.8%	8.0%	13.5%
Respond with military means, even if alone	8.8%	4.8%	31.4%	4.2%	7.6%	10.7%
Don't know	3.3%	4.2%	2.0%	0.0%	4.0%	2.2%

Source: Public Agenda and Tomás Rivera Policy Institute, New York and Claremont, Calif., 1998.

Table 2.8: Military Coup Scenario

A Latin American democracy faces a military coup and the legally elected government requested U.S. help to resist the coup.

Should the U.S.:	Hispanic leaders	Mexican American	Cuban American	Puerto Rican	Native born	Foreign born
Stay out	8.4%	6.9%	5.9%	12.5%	7.6%	9.6%
Respond with diplomatic and economic means, but only in cooperation with other Latin American countries	39.9%	43.9%	23.5%	39.6%	37.1%	43.8%
Respond with diplomatic and economic means, even if alone	14.1%	15.3%	13.7%	14.6%	16.0%	11.2%
Respond with military means, but only in cooperation with other Latin American countries	24.4%	23.3%	29.4%	22.9%	26.9%	20.8%
Respond with military means, even if alone	8.4%	5.8%	23.5%	6.3%	6.9%	10.7%
Don't know	2.2%	2.6%	2.0%	2.1%	2.5%	1.7%

Source: Public Agenda and Tomás Rivera Policy Institute, New York and Claremont, Calif., 1998.

United States with illegal drugs. Hispanic leaders in general again show a greater propensity toward diplomatic or economic means to resolve the issue; however, they also show a greater willingness to use these tools unilaterally without the cooperation of Latin American allies. Cuban Americans again demonstrate a willingness to use unilateral military intervention (table 2.11).

The final scenario involves political and social upheaval in Mexico resulting in massive immigration into the United States. As with the previous scenario, Hispanic leaders in general display a greater propensity toward diplomatic or economic means to resolve the issue. Once again, they also show a greater willingness to use these tools unilaterally without the cooperation of Latin

Table 2.9: Human Rights Violation Scenario

A Latin American government engages in systematic torture and violations of the human rights of its population.

Should the U.S.:	Hispanic leaders	Mexican American	Cuban American	Puerto Rican	Native born	Foreign born
Stay out	4.4%	4.8%	3.9%	4.2%	4.4%	4.5%
Respond with diplomatic and economic means, but only in cooperation with other Latin American countries	37.7%	39.2%	21.6%	45.8%	34.9%	41.6%
Respond with diplomatic and economic means, even if alone	36.8%	37.0%	45.1%	37.5%	41.1%	30.3%
Respond with military means, but only in cooperation with other Latin American countries	10.6%	8.5%	11.8%	8.3%	9.8%	11.8%
Respond with military means, even if alone	7.0%	6.9%	15.7%	2.1%	6.2%	8.4%
Don't know	0.7%	1.1%	0.0%	0.0%	0.7%	0.6%

Source: Public Agenda and Tomás Rivera Policy Institute, New York and Claremont, Calif., 1998.

American allies. Cuban Americans again express a greater willingness to use unilateral military intervention (see table 2.12).

These scenarios serve to highlight the conditions and foreign policy instruments most preferred by Hispanic leaders. In general, they prefer the multilateral use of diplomatic and economic instruments to unilateral political-military instruments. Two exceptions emerge. First, Mexico is the only country in which the Hispanic leadership, regardless of national origin, is most likely to favor the use of political and economic instruments without the cooperation of the United

Table 2.10: Fidel Castro Dies Scenario

Fidel Castro dies, chaos and fighting break out in Cuba, and a flood of refugees begins to pour into Florida.

Should the U.S.:	Hispanic leaders	Mexican American	Cuban American	Puerto Rican	Native born	Foreign born
Stay out	6.8%	7.4%	2.0%	4.2%	7.3%	6.2%
Respond with diplomatic and economic means, but only in cooperation with other Latin American countries	34.4%	36.5%	17.6%	43.8%	33.1%	36.0%
Respond with diplomatic and economic means, even if alone	25.3%	30.2%	21.6%	20.8%	29.5%	19.1%
Respond with military means, but only in cooperation with other Latin American countries	11.7%	11.6%	11.8%	14.6%	10.5%	13.5%
Respond with military means, even if alone	15.9%	9.5%	45.1%	6.3%	13.5%	19.7%
Don't know	2.4%	1.6%	0.0%	4.2%	2.5%	2.2%

Source: Public Agenda and Tomás Rivera Policy Institute, New York and Claremont, Calif., 1998.

States' Latin American allies. The second involves the Cuban American population. Perhaps out of historical experience, this group is more willing to use unilateral political-military intervention in order to achieve a desired policy objective particularly when the scenario involves Cuba.

The fact that Hispanic leaders are willing to support unilateral policies, including military intervention, for strategically important countries suggests a disconnection with the interests of the homeland. The principle of nonintervention is a cornerstone in Latin American foreign policy. Latin Americans have enshrined it in several articles of the Organization of American States' charter. For example,

Table 2.11: Drug Kingpin in Mexico Scenario

A drug kingpin under indictment in U.S. court is living openly in Mexico, where he is protected by corrupt officials and runs a massive operation smuggling drugs across the border.

Should the U.S.:	Hispanic leaders	Mexican American	Cuban American	Puerto Rican	Native born	Foreign born
Stay out	5.9%	5.8%	3.9%	4.2%	5.5%	6.7%
Respond with diplomatic and economic means, but only in cooperation with other Latin American countries	23.8%	24.9%	17.6%	29.2%	21.8%	26.4%
Respond with diplomatic and economic means, even if alone	40.1%	40.2%	35.3%	41.7%	44.0%	34.3%
Respond with military means, but only in cooperation with other Latin American countries	9.3%	9.5%	13.7%	2.1%	8.7%	10.1%
Respond with military means, even if alone	15.2%	13.2%	27.5%	14.6%	13.5%	18.0%
Don't know	2.4%	3.2%	0.0%	6.3%	3.6%	0.6%

Source: Public Agenda and Tomás Rivera Policy Institute, New York and Claremont, Calif., 1998.

Article 18 explicitly states that "no State has the right to intervene directly or indirectly, for any reason whatever, in the internal or external affairs of any other state" (Pastor 1992; Weston, Falk, D'Amato 1990). Moreover, the principle of nonintervention is explicitly stated in many of the Latin American constitutions. For example, Article 33 of the Mexican Constitution explicitly prohibits the involvement of foreigners in affairs of state.

What reactions to these scenarios suggest, then, is that Hispanic leaders' foreign policy perspectives are not congruent with the official perspectives of most Latin American governments and intellectuals. The former reflect an interest

Table 2.12: Political Chaos in Mexico Scenario

Political chaos and social upheaval break out in Mexico, resulting in a dramatic increase in the number of illegal/undocumented immigrants crossing the border from Mexico into the U.S.

Should the U.S.:	Hispanic leaders	Mexican American	Cuban American	Puerto Rican	Native born	Foreign born
Stay out	5.9%	5.3%	2.0%	8.3%	5.8%	6.2%
Respond with diplomatic and economic means, but only in cooperation with other Latin American countries	29.1%	32.3%	19.6%	31.3%	28.7%	29.2%
Respond with diplomatic and economic means, even if alone	40.1%	47.1%	29.4%	47.9%	45.8%	31.5%
Respond with military means, but only in cooperation with other Latin American countries	7.0%	3.7%	9.8%	6.3%	6.5%	7.9%
Respond with military means, even if alone	13.2%	7.4%	37.3%	4.2%	9.1%	19.7%
Don't know	1.3%	1.6%	2.0%	0.0%	1.1%	1.7%

Source: Public Agenda and Tomás Rivera Policy Institute, New York and Claremont, Calif., 1998.

in advancing the interests of the United States rather than those of the homeland, as Huntington and others would allege.

Conclusion

The study of diasporas and ethnic lobbies in the United States has generated widespread interest among researchers particularly with the end of the Cold War.

A debate is currently raging among academics and foreign policy scholars regarding the rising influence of ethnic lobbies on U.S. foreign policy. Although much has been written on diasporas such as the Jewish American, the Greek American, and the Cuban American, the growing demographic and political influence of other Hispanic groups has also drawn academics to examine how these new diasporas might influence U.S. foreign policy.

This book seeks to enter the current debate regarding the nexus between ethnic groups and U.S. foreign policy. In this chapter we have sought to demystify the Hispanic diaspora by analyzing a nationwide survey of Hispanic leaders and their perspectives on the nation's foreign policy goals for the post–Cold War era. Based on the results of the survey, we conclude that Hispanic leaders are primarily domestically oriented and that their foreign policy priorities are similar in many ways to those of leaders in general. Despite the greater saliency of domestic over foreign policy issues, Hispanic leaders are not isolationist. In fact, the majority favor an active role for the United States in world affairs. Not surprisingly, Hispanic leaders show a greater interest in elevating the importance of Latin America than that of other parts of the world; however, not all Latin American countries are equal in this regard. No matter the respondent's national origin or nativity, Mexico is the centerpiece for Hispanic leaders. In crisis scenarios involving Mexico, Hispanic leaders overwhelmingly favor unilateral action, including military intervention. These attitudes regarding Mexico's strategic importance are consistent with the attitudes of non-U.S. leaders in general. In some ways, Huntington and others are correct in assuming that ethnic groups are concerned with their historical homelands. This does not mean, however, that these interests are inimical to U.S. interests. Both Cuban American and Mexican American leaders reveal a greater interest in following developments and events in their homelands; however, Hispanic leaders' foreign policy preferences do not indicate transnational loyalties. They are interested in becoming involved in shaping U.S.–Latin American relations, although not to the exclusion of other regions. Tellingly, Latino leaders are quick to point out that they have no interest in pursuing policies that may contravene or compromise U.S. interests.

Notes

1. The leadership sample involved 383 individual interviews conducted by telephone between October 26 and December 7, 1994. The sample included Americans in senior positions with knowledge of international affairs. Interviewees came in roughly equal proportions from the House of Representatives, the Senate, and the administration. Leaders were drawn from the Foreign Relations, Foreign Affairs, and Armed Services committees of Congress and from international offices in the State, Treasury, Defense, and other federal

departments. Leaders were also drawn from the business community (international vice presidents of large corporations), the media (editors and columnists of major newspapers and magazines, television and radio news directors, and network newscasters), academia (presidents of and scholars from major colleges and universities), and private foreign policy institutions. A smaller number of leaders was drawn from national labor unions, churches, and special-interest groups relevant to foreign policy. John E. Rielley, *American Public Opinion and U.S. Foreign Policy*, Chicago Council on Foreign Relations, 1995, 2-3.

References

de la Garza, Rodolfo O. 1987. "U.S. Foreign Policy and the Mexican American Political Agenda." In *Ethnic Groups and U.S. Foreign Policy*, edited by Mohammed Ahari. Westport, Conn.: Greenwood Press, 101–114.

Fernández, Damián. 1987. "From Little Havana to Washington, D.C., Cuban-Americans and U.S. Foreign Policy." In *Ethnic Groups and U.S. Foreign Policy*, edited by Mohammed Ahari. Westport, Conn.: Greenwood Press, 1987, 115-134.

Huntington, Samuel P. 1997. "The Erosion of American Interests." *Foreign Affairs*, September/October, 28–49.

Jelen, Ted G. 1994. "Religion and Foreign Policy Attitudes: Exploring the Effects of Denomination and Doctrine." *American Politics Quarterly* 22, no. 3 (July): 382B–400.

Pastor, Robert A. 1992. *Whirlpool: U.S. Foreign Policy toward Latin America and the Caribbean.* Princeton: Princeton University Press.

Public Agenda and Tomás Rivera Policy Institute. 1998. *Here to Stay: The Domestic and Foreign Policy Priorities of Latino Leaders.* New York and Claremont, Calif.

Schlesinger, Arthur. 1991. *The Disuniting of America.* New York: W. W. Norton.

Togeby, Lisa. 1994. "The Gender Gap in Foreign Policy Attitudes." *Journal of Peace Research* 31, no. 4 (November): 375–392.

Weston, Burns, H., Richard A. Falk, and Anthony D'Amato. 1990. *Basic Documents in International Law and World Order.* St. Paul, Minn.: West Publishing Company.

3
Family Ties and Ethnic Lobbies

Rodolfo O. de la Garza,
Harry P. Pachon, Manuel Orozco
and Adrián D. Pantoja

The ideas and issues that shaped this research were developed over several years.[1] In February 1995, in collaboration with the Stanley Foundation, the Tomás Rivera Policy Institute (TRPI) convened a conference on Latinos, global change, and American foreign policy. The resulting report concluded that Latinos in the United States are positioned to play a key role in shaping U.S. foreign policy vis-à-vis Latin American countries. A second conference, sponsored in May 1995 by TRPI and the Stanley Foundation, considered the extent to which Southwestern states shape U.S. foreign policy. The conference report highlighted the role that Latinos might play in foreign policymaking, particularly in the Western Hemisphere. Following on the heels of these conferences, TRPI—with generous support from the Andrew W. Mellon Foundation—launched a research initiative in the field of foreign policy and Western Hemispheric relations. In July 1996, TRPI expanded the scope of the initiative with additional support from the Ford Foundation.

43

Broadly speaking, this study aims to ascertain whether and how Latinos in the United States influence relationships between the United States and five of its Latin American neighbors: Colombia, the Dominican Republic, El Salvador, Guatemala, and Mexico.[2] More specifically, it examines the extent to which individuals and groups with ties to these five countries affect cross-national relations and foreign policies adopted by the U.S. government. By *relations* we mean the sum total of all links and interactions that are established between nongovernmental actors (NGOs) from two nation-states. These nonofficial links are of course affected by formal international policies but are not the sole and direct product of them. Although international policies are the result of an institutionalized policymaking process, international relations are affected by numerous other agents and forces that are not formally under the complete control and command of any state. In very sketchy terms, we may say that *policies* are part of a formal international system of interactions, whereas *relations* encompass a much broader spectrum of processes that may be termed *spontaneous*. The great migratory flows that characterize our contemporary global society are a good example of such *spontaneous* interactions, which are affected but not entirely shaped by international or domestic policies. Cross-national relations are complex phenomena that have become salient in the last ten years—particularly since the end of the Cold War—and that are still in the process of acquiring more definite contours.

The research addresses the following questions:

1. How do elites in Latin America understand the role of U.S. Latinos (native-born and immigrants) in shaping policies and relations between home countries and the United States? What impact do U.S. Latinos have in their countries of origin?

2. What kinds of policies do Latin American governments implement vis-à-vis Latino communities in the United States?

3. Do links exist between U.S. Latino organizations and Latin American nongovernmental organizations, or NGOs? If so, how strong and enduring are they?

4. In what ways are U.S. Latino organizations involved in foreign policymaking in the United States? Are Latino organizations able to influence policy decisions, and if so, which actors are influential?

Major Findings

The results presented here should be viewed from two perspectives. First, they should be seen as an independent description and assessment of how the multifaceted relationships between U.S. Latinos and a wide range of individuals and organizations in selected Latin American countries are affecting U.S. policies toward those countries. They thus provide a unique insight into Hispanic influence on those policies. Second, they should be seen as part of the larger research initiative regarding Latino involvement in foreign policy that includes the Latino FSO survey described in chapter 1 and the survey of Latino elites described in chapter 2. To set the findings of this chapter in context, we will therefore begin by briefly reviewing the results of the survey of Latino elites.

The survey of Hispanic leaders, *Here to Stay* (Farkas, de la Garza, et al. 1998) reveals two distinct patterns in the way Latino leaders view international issues. First, the leaders who responded to the survey are much more concerned with domestic issues than with international problems. This pattern also holds for those leaders, both the native born and immigrants, who participated in the present study. Second, despite the saliency they attach to domestic matters, Latino leaders are keenly interested in international issues: Almost 90 percent indicate that the United States should take an active part in world affairs.

Hispanic leaders are especially interested in Latin American issues, and most have extensive personal and professional linkages to Latin America. More than half (52%) have participated in a wide range of activities regarding U.S.–Latin American affairs, almost 90 percent closely follow events in Latin America, 92 percent have actually been there, and 59 percent have traveled there within the past twelve months. Not surprisingly, then, the great majority (85%) of Hispanic leaders think the United States should pay more attention to relations with Latin America.

Together these findings suggest that, on the one hand, Latinos attitudes toward foreign policy and international relations are like those of most Americans. That is, international issues are not their top priority. Nonetheless, like other Americans, Latinos are internationally engaged and want the nation to remain active in world affairs. Unlike other Americans, however, Latinos focus primarily on Latin America. Although this may not be surprising, the depth and breadth of their engagement with Latin America are at least noteworthy, suggesting that as Latinos become more politically influential, they may seek to expand or alter the nation's international priorities by making Latin America a first-tier concern.

How likely are Latinos to do so? What specific policies will they advocate? Will they be asked to advance home country interests at the expense of U.S. concerns, or will the U.S. government call on them to assist with advancing U.S. policies that home country governments may oppose? How likely are they to draw on their experiences in the United States to press home country governments to adopt major political and economic reforms even if the U.S. and home country governments disagree? There is no clear answer to these questions. Nonetheless, we can begin to clarify many of the issues they raise by examining the current relationships between major Hispanic populations and their countries of origin. Items 1–7 summarize what the present study has found about those relationships:

1. Immigration from Mexico, El Salvador, Guatemala, Colombia, and the Dominican Republic has soared since the 1980s, creating substantial new communities of Guatemalans, Salvadorans, and Colombians and greatly enlarging those of Mexicans and Dominicans. Such communities have developed strong social and economic links with their home societies.

2. Home country governments responded to the surge in emigration by making efforts to establish formal relations with emigrant communities. Mexico in the late 1980s was the first to initiate official outreach programs, and by the mid-1990s all five of the study countries except Guatemala had launched similar efforts.

3. Despite widespread interest in international and home country affairs, the overwhelming majority of Latino organizational leaders focus primarily on issues affecting the well-being of Latinos within the United States, such as employment, education, and immigration. This is true both for leaders of organizations serving immigrants and for those with native-born constituencies. Personal interviews and a national survey of Latino leaders both support this finding.

4. We uncovered few examples of Latino organizations directly attempting to influence foreign policy processes. When these organizations have engaged in foreign policy, they have done so either autonomously (i.e., not in response to mobilization by home country governments) or, as the North American Free Trade Agreement (NAFTA) and Fast-Track congressional votes illustrate, at the request of U.S. government officials. However, individual Latinos were hired by the Mexican government to lobby on behalf of NAFTA.

5. U.S. officials and officials from the governments of the countries studied here generally agree that increasing trade, promoting investment, and strengthening democracy are the key issues in the respective bilateral relationships. All the Latino leaders we interviewed support these goals strongly, and our poll of Hispanic elites indicates that more than half believe trade, democracy, and human rights should be the pillars of the country's foreign policy. Thus, even if Hispanic leaders were mobilized by home country governments to lobby on their behalf, they would simultaneously be lobbying on behalf of the official policy preferences of the United States Department of State (USDOS).

6. Latinos have mobilized around immigration issues, with a focus on protecting immigrant access to social services and on preventing the deportation of Central American immigrants. Thus, even though home country governments have encouraged such involvement, Latinos' mobilization reflects their domestic rather than foreign policy concerns. Immigration is therefore a clear example of an *intermestic* policy—that is, it intrinsically combines domestic and international dimensions (Gress 1996, Lowenthal 1992)—and so when Latinos engage it for domestic reasons they simultaneously become involved in foreign policy and international issues.

7. No single pattern describes how home country societies view emigrants or how interested their governments are in developing relations with emigrants.[3] Instead, societal views vary from highly positive to negative or indifferent, whereas governmental interest ranges from intense and well developed to undeveloped and uncertain. Overall, the most positive and comprehensive relations are those between the Dominican Republic and its émigrés, but it is Salvadoran society and its government that give greatest priority to relations with emigrants. The least-developed relations are those involving Guatemala and Colombia. Mexico's are the most complex, mixing elaborate governmental initiatives with negative societal ties.

We discuss these findings in detail below.

Methodology

We based our data collection on the premise that *four factors* seem to determine the extent to which Latinos are establishing links with Latin America and/or exerting foreign policy influence in the United States. One is the demographic weight that Latino communities carry in those U.S. states where they are concentrated.[4] Another is the set of national perceptions (both official and *informal* or *spontaneous*) that Latin Americans have of their emigrants and the way those perceptions influence Latinos' mobilization vis-à-vis their countries of origin. A third is the policy priorities of Latino leaders[5] and the way those priorities influence the level of Latino involvement with Latin American–U.S. relations and policies. And a fourth is the official outreach by Latin American governments to their conationals or descendants in the United States, which can reveal important trends in the way official circles view the emigrants' role and are likely to influence Latino attempts to shape U.S. foreign policy. We then gathered the data for this report in four ways:

1. We carried out an extensive review of the relevant literature and compiled a bibliographic database covering more than 400 titles.
2. We gathered demographic and economic information from the U.S. national census and the World Bank.
3. We conducted structured, person-to-person interviews with diplomatic officials (stationed in the United States) from the five study countries, government and NGO representatives in Latin America, Latino elites in the United States, and USDOS officials in Washington and in U.S. embassies in each study country.[6]
4. Together with Public Agenda, we implemented a mail survey targeting Latino leaders in the United States. The survey yielded a sample of 454 questionnaires returned out of the 1,380 that had been sent.[7]

The personal interviews, which lasted from around 45 minutes to three hours, were structured around semi-open questionnaires that varied slightly according to type of interviewee. However, they all covered some common topics in order to facilitate comparisons not only among different categories of interviewees (e.g., NGO representatives, embassy and consular officials, business leaders, and academics), but also among various cities in the United States and among countries in Latin America (please see tables 3.1 and 3.2).

Latinos and U.S.–Latin American Relations

Latinos in the United States

Demographics

The Latino population of the United States has grown substantially since the 1980s, mainly as a consequence of immigration driven by the political crises and economic decline that have plagued Latin America since the 1970s as well as by high birthrates. Specifically, more than 50 percent of Mexican, Dominican, Central American, and South American immigrants to the United States arrived after 1980 (table 3.3). Nearly 70 percent of the Central Americans entered during the 1980s. The high growth rate is expected to continue well into the next century (table 3.4).

As of 1990, the vast majority of people of Colombian, Dominican, Guatemalan, and Salvadoran descent living in the United States were foreign-born (table 3.5A). Only among people of Mexican descent did U.S. natives outnumber (by a

Table 3.1: Institutional Affiliations of Interviewees in the U.S.

Institution	Latino NGO representatives	Consulate officials	Embassy officials	USDOS officials	Other[a]	Total
Cities						
Austin	6	–	–	–	–	6
Chicago	8	4	–	–	–	12
Houston	4	4	–	–	–	8
Los Angeles	7	2	–	–	–	9
Miami	11	2	–	–	–	13
New York	8	5	–	–	–	13
San Antonio	1	–	–	–	–	1
Washington, D.C.	4	5	3	6	2	20
Total	49	22	3	6	2	82

[a] A U.S. congressman and a university professor.

Table 3.2: Institutional Affiliations of Interviewees in Latin America

Groups[a]	Govt. officials	NGO reps	Academics	Business leaders	Embassy personnel	USDOS officials	Other[b]	Total
Countries								
Colombia	1	4	1	1	2	3	2	14
Dominican Republic	2	2	1	1	2	3	3	14
El Salvador	4	6	4	2	3	5	2	26
Guatemala	2	5	3	1	–	2	1	15
Mexico	3	2	–	1	3	4	4	17
Total	12	19	9	6	11	17	12	86

[a] Numerous respondents held several of these positions over time. Here they are grouped according to the position held at the time of the interviews.
[b] Includes politicians and other notable individuals.

Table 3.3: Decade of Entry into the United States for Selected Foreign-Born Hispanic Groups

	% of current population that arrived in U.S. pre-1960	% of current population that arrived in U.S. 1960–69	% of current population that arrived in U.S. 1970–79	% of current population that arrived in U.S. 1980–89
Total Hispanic	6.80	15.00	27.50	50.70
Central American	2.90	7.20	20.10	69.90
Dominican	2.80	17.20	26.60	53.50
Mexican	7.90	10.70	31.00	50.40
South American	4.10	18.30	26.50	51.10

Source: U.S. Bureau of the Census, *1990 Census of Population.*

Table 3.4: Population Projections for Hispanics and Non-Hispanic Whites, 1980 to 2050 (in thousands)

Year	Total U.S. population	Number of Hispanics	Hispanic % of population	Number of non-Hispanic Whites	Non-Hispanic White % of population
1980	226,546	14,609	6	180,906	80
1985	237,924	18,368	8	184,945	78
1990	248,718	22,354	9	188,306	76
1995	262,755	26,994	10	193,523	74
2000	271,237	30,393	11	195,505	72
2005	276,990	33,527	12	195,589	71
2010	281,468	36,652	13	194,628	69
2020	288,807	43,287	15	191,047	66
2030	291,070	49,834	17	183,295	63
2040	287,685	56,104	20	171,054	59
2050	282,524	62,230	22	157,701	56

Source: U.S. Department of Commerce, *Population Projections of the United States by Age, Sex, Race and Hispanic Origin, 1995–2050* (1996, 1).

two-to-one margin) immigrants. The 1980 census reveals that at that time an even higher percentage of people of Mexican ancestry in the United States were native-born, nearly 75 percent (table 5B). It is not possible to examine the other nationality populations individually for 1980, since the census did not differentiate among "other Hispanics." However, as of 1980, 60 percent of "other Hispanics"—a category including Central and South Americans but not Cubans or Puerto Ricans—had been born in the United States (table 3.5B).

We note too that the five countries under study differ significantly with respect to the percentage of their nationals living in the United States (table 3.6). As of 1990, less than one percent of all Colombians were living in the United States, whereas about nine percent of all Salvadorans were. As the population of nationals living outside the home country grows, so does the importance of linkages such as remittances to the home country economy, as discussed below.

Geographic Distribution

Although Latinos have spread across the continental United States, most are concentrated in five states—California, Florida, Illinois, New York, and Texas (table 3.7). As of 1990, nearly 3 million Latinos who could trace their origins to our five study countries lived in California; the second-highest number, 940,000, lived in Texas. California was home to the vast majority of Guatemalans, Mexicans, and Salvadorans, whereas most Dominicans had chosen to live in New York State. Colombians were more equally distributed, with most living in New York and Florida and a substantial number in California.

Socioeconomic Profile

The five nationality groups vary by occupational status. As of 1990, nearly 9 percent of Colombians who emigrated to the United States were in professional occupations, whereas only about 5 percent of Dominicans and less than 4 percent of Guatemalans, Salvadorans, and Mexicans were (table 3.8). In terms of total labor force participation, about 75 percent of Colombian, Guatemalan, and Salvadoran immigrants were in the U.S. labor force in 1990, as were a slightly smaller percentage of Mexicans and Dominicans.

Economic attainment correlates to some extent with nativity (table 3.9). In 1989, for instance, the median household income for all persons born in the United States was slightly more than $30,100, whereas for all immigrants it was about $28,300 and for Latin American and Caribbean immigrants it was about $24,400. Differences among specific nationalities are also significant. In

Table 3.5A: Selected Native and Foreign-Born Populations in the United States, 1990

Ancestry	Total native born	Total foreign born	% Native born	% Foreign born
Colombian and Colombian descent	97, 657	281,069	25.70	74.20
Dominican and Dominican descent	153,078	367,073	29.40	70.50
Guatemalan and Guatemalan descent	52,783	251,996	17.30	82.60
Mexican and Mexican descent	8,933,371	4,459,837	66.00	33.00
Salvadoran and Salvadoran descent	106,405	458,676	18.80	81.10

Source: U.S. Bureau of the Census, 1990 Census of Population.

Table 3.5B: Selected Native and Foreign-Born Populations in the United States, 1980

	Native born	Foreign born	% Native born	% Foreign born
Mexican and Mexican descent	6,421,930	2,256,702	73.90	26.00
"Other Hispanic" [a]	1,887,036	1,226,831	60.00	39.00

Source: U.S. Bureau of the Census, 1980 Census of Populations.
[a] Excludes Cubans, Mexicans, and Puerto Ricans.

1989, Colombian immigrants registered the highest median household income (more than $29,000) while Dominicans had the lowest (slightly less than $20,000). Colombians were also much less likely than Dominicans, Guatemalans, Mexicans, or Salvadorans to be in poverty. Although the poverty rate for Colombians hovered at about 15 percent, the rates for the other four groups were at least 25 percent and, in the case of Dominicans, reached 30 percent.[8]

Table 3.6: Country Populations and Number
of Selected Hispanic Foreign-Born Nationals in the U.S.

National origin	Total national population		Number of foreign-born nationals living in U.S.		Foreign-born nationals as % of native country's total population	
	1990	1994	1990	1994	1990	1994
Colombia	32,300,000	34,545,000	286,000	na [a]	0.89	na
Dominican Republic	7,170,000	7,769,000	348,000	515,000	4.85	6.63
El Salvador	5,172,000	5,641,000	465,000	701,000	8.99	12.43
Guatemala	9,197,000	10,322,000	226,000	na	2.46	na
Mexico	81,250,000	88,431,000	4,298,000	6,779,000	5.29	7.67

Source: U.S. Bureau of the Census, *1990 Census of Population* and *Current Population Survey* (1994); World Bank Tables, 1995.
[a] na = not available.

Issues in U.S.–Latin American Relations

From the declaration of the Monroe Doctrine in 1823 to the end of the Cold War, U.S. interests in the Western Hemisphere were primarily strategic. U.S. policies were designed to ensure the country's political and economic supremacy in a region viewed as constantly under threat from external powers (Hartlyn, Schoultz, and Varas 1992). Until World War II, U.S. policies aimed at countering European powers. Afterward, they focused on limiting perceived Soviet challenges to U.S. supremacy. Problems in Latin American countries that were related to political and economic inequalities were typically framed in terms of the "East-West" conflict. U.S. policymakers frequently saw challenges to the status quo in the Western Hemisphere as Soviet-inspired.

With the collapse of the Soviet Union in 1991, new challenges and themes in U.S.–Latin American relations have emerged. The most important of these are democratization, human rights, trade and investment, drugs, and immigration (Molineau 1990). It is important to note that these priorities resonate strongly among U.S. Latino leaders: well over half (56%) of those in our mail survey gave top priority to increasing trade with Latin America, and a little over half (52%) wanted support for democracy and human rights to be a central pillar of U.S. policy toward the region. These themes are highly compatible with official U.S. hemispheric policies.

Table 3.7: Distribution of Selected Latino Nationality Groups in the United States, 1990

Household	California	Florida	Illinois	New York	Texas	Washington D.C.	Total # residing in 5 states and D.C.	Total # residing in USA	Percent residing in 5 states and D.C.
Colombian	30,680	66,614	7,331	82,767	12,430	799	200,621	286,000	70
Dominican	3,535	23,373	1,217	241,941	1,760	1,103	272,929	348,000	78
Guatemalan	135,875	11,480	12,493	17,883	10,366	1,175	189,272	226,000	84
Mexican	2,474,148	55,316	281,651	43,505	907,432	1,034	3,763,086	4,298,000	87
Salvadoran	280,781	10,142	5,055	37,177	16,366	19,276	368,797	465,000	79
Total	2,925,019	166,925	307,747	423,273	942,354	13,387	4,778,705	5,623,000	85

Source: U.S. Bureau of the Census, *1990 Census of Population.*

Table 3.8: Labor Force Participation
of Selected Hispanic Immigrant Groups, 1990

Country of birth	# of individuals in U.S. labor force	% of immigrant group in U.S. labor force	% of immigrant group in professional occupations
Colombia	286,124	73.70	8.80
Dominican Republic	347,858	63.80	5.20
El Salvador	486,433	76.30	2.40
Guatemala	225,739	75.70	3.30
Mexico	4,298,014	69.70	2.60

Source: U.S. Bureau of the Census, *1990 Census of Population*.

Table 3.9: Median Household Income and Poverty Rates
for Selected Immigrant Nationalities in the United States, 1989

Country or region	# of persons	Median household income	Poverty rate (%)
Total U.S. native born	228,942,557	$30,176	12.7
All immigrants	19,767,316	$28,314	18.2
All Latin American and Caribbean immigrants	8,416,924	$24,385	24.3
Colombian immigrants	286,124	$29,139	15.3
Dominican immigrants	347,858	$19,996	30.0
El Salvadoran immigrants	485,433	$23,533	24.9
Guatemalan immigrants	225,739	$24,362	25.8
Mexican immigrants	4,298,014	$21,926	29.7

Source: U.S. Bureau of the Census, *1990 Census of Population*.

Consolidating new democracies sits high on the agenda for many Latin American countries. Latin American and U.S. officials have promoted peace processes and assisted with the transition to political democracy in El Salvador, Nicaragua, and, most recently, Guatemala (Muñoz 1996, 194). Multilateral intervention in Haiti against the Raoul Cedras military coup and condemnation by the Organization of American States (OAS) of Peruvian President Alberto Fujimori's "coup" are evidence that democratization remains a foreign policy priority in Western Hemispheric relations (Muñoz 1996, 195–96). The great majority of Latino leaders share this priority (Farkas. de la Garza, et al. 1998); a Hispanic NGO leader from Chicago articulated their perspective well when he said, "This is a democratic hemisphere, so we need fair elections and the rule of law."

A second basic priority for Latin American countries is attaining high rates of economic growth and development comparable to those in the United States and Western Europe. A number of countries have implemented policies to combat poverty and inequality and to end Latin America's perceived dependence on developed nations (Van Klaveren 1992, 39). Recent strategies have abandoned inward-oriented industrialization policies in favor of policies aimed at promoting exports, privatization, foreign investment, and regional economic integration through multinational agreements such as NAFTA and MERCOSUR (*Mercado Común del Sur,* the Southern Common Market) (Fishlow and Haggard 1992; Jaguaribe 1991). In this context, Latin America continues to regard the United States as a major trading partner. U.S. Latinos have not remained indifferent to the rising importance of interhemispheric trade. They expressed as much to us many times in the course of our personal interviews, and our survey found that nearly 70 percent of respondents felt the United States should extend free trade with other Latin American countries following the NAFTA model. Moreover, 77 percent of Hispanic leaders in our poll thought the future would hold greater interdependence between the United States and Latin America.

Not surprisingly, 88 percent of them said the United States should pay more attention to its relations with Latin America. Their view, which was also expressed during interviews, is supported by the rising economic importance of Latin America—especially Mexico—within overall U.S. foreign trade. In fact, Mexico has become almost the second U.S. trading partner, in close competition with Japan (table 3.10 and figure 3.1).

Drug trafficking has also been identified as a major hemispheric issue (Van Klaveren 1992, 29). In fact, the "war on drugs" has overshadowed other security concerns. U.S. and Latin American leaders appear to agree that "drug production, smuggling, and abuse constitute a significant threat to national security and societal well-being throughout the hemisphere" (Tokatlian and Bagley

Table 3.10: Top Five U.S. Trading Partners

Country	Total in billions of U.S.$ (for the month of January 1998)
Canada	25.40
Japan	14.64
Mexico	13.22
China	6.66
United Kingdom	5.57

Source: U.S. Bureau of the Census, International Trade Statistics, 1998.

1990, 214). In bilateral and multilateral relationships, the United States has pursued a variety of counter-drug trafficking strategies (Tokatlian and Bagley 1990, 231). Although Latino leaders agree that the drug traffic is a significant problem, they do not think that it should be a top priority of U.S. foreign policy. Their views are quite similar to those of other American leaders. A recent Gallup poll found that 85 percent of the public think controlling drugs is a very important goal, but only 57 percent of U.S. leaders and 54 percent of the Latino leaders in our survey share that opinion. While the views of Hispanic leaders may differ from the general public's, they do not differ much from those of U.S. leaders overall.

Figure 3.1: Graph of U.S. Exports to Selected Countries
(as percentage from total exports)

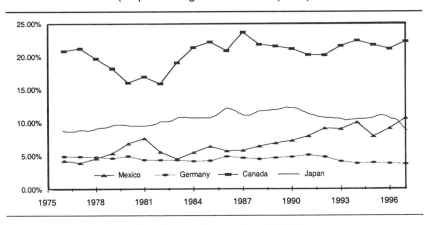

Source: International Monetary Fund. Direction of Trade Statistics, 1980–1998.

Transnational migration too, has become an increasingly contentious issue in the hemisphere (Bach and Meissner 1990, 262; Castañeda 1994, 35–37; Ullman 1995, 76–80; Van Klaveren 1992, 29). Some observers argue that migration may come to overshadow other foreign policy concerns. As Robert A. Pastor notes: "More than one-third of all immigration since [1960], and 86 percent of the immigration to the United States from Latin America and the Caribbean, has come from the Caribbean Basin. In the long term, these transnational human bonds may prove more influential in shaping inter-American relations than have strategic concerns" (1992, 25).

In short, U.S.–Latin American relations have moved from a narrow focus on East-West security issues to a paradigm dominated by more diverse concerns. While the issues have become more varied and complex, foreign policymaking—once considered best left to elite government officials—is now subject to influence and challenges from various nongovernmental interests, including ethnic groups (Clough 1994, Huntington 1996). The extent to which the latter are able to influence policy, we argue, will depend substantially on the relationship between emigrant communities and their home countries. To understand that relationship, we must examine the foreign policy and international perspectives of these diaspora communities, the ways such communities are viewed by officials in the home countries, and the links between home country institutions and emigrants. Our survey of Hispanic elites, *Here to Stay,* examined the first of these topics. This report examines the other two.

Perceptions and Impacts

The role that "diasporas"[9] may play in shaping U.S. policy toward their home countries depends on how the diasporas view those countries and on how the countries' governments and societies perceive them. Diasporas may mobilize in response to home country issues independent of any government efforts to mobilize them and regardless of how they are perceived by their home country societies. However, efforts to mobilize are likely to be influenced by how the home country's society and government perceive emigrants, the extent to which they have established or attempted to establish relationships with the emigrants, and the types of institutions involved. If emigrants are ignored or viewed negatively, for example, they may be less likely to mobilize on behalf of the home country than if they are held in high esteem there. Curiously, studies of ethnic involvement in American foreign policy do not systematically consider home country attitudes toward and interactions with emigrants. Our research suggests this is a major oversight.

As noted above, we interviewed leaders from the press, government, political parties, businesses, human rights organizations, universities, and independent research institutions about the ways their respective societies and agencies view and interact with emigrants. We conducted our interviews in the capital cities of the five countries under study and in Guadalajara, which is Mexico's second-largest city and capital of the state of Jalisco. Respondents were asked to draw on their institutional and personal experiences to discuss four themes:

- Societal perceptions of emigrants
- The impact of emigrants on national political, cultural, and economic life
- Efforts by governmental and nongovernmental organizations to develop relations with emigrants or U.S. Latinos in general
- Efforts to mobilize emigrants on issues involving the home country's relations with the United States

We should note that the responses did not differ greatly among the respondents from any single country on any issue, but they did differ greatly from country to country, as will be seen.

Societal Perceptions of Emigrants

Emigrants' Visibility in the Home Country

Societal perceptions are defined as how much and what kind of attention emigrants receive. In El Salvador and, to a lesser degree, in the Dominican Republic, emigrants are the focus of continuous attention from a wide array of private and public institutions. In both countries, the press regularly publishes stories on emigrants and on migrants who have returned, and newspapers carry advertising for emigrant businesses, advertising that not only promotes the interests of specific establishments but, more important for the purposes of this study, also serves to inform Salvadorans and Dominicans that many of their compatriots in the United States are enjoying economic success.

Universities, independent research centers, government agencies, political parties, and business organizations in both countries also deal regularly with emigrant-related issues. Salvadoran political leaders and researchers, for example, are engaged in an ongoing public discussion on how to encourage the use of remittances for investment rather than personal consumption (López and Seligson

1990, Siri and Abelardo Delgado 1995). In the Dominican Republic, business, government, and academic leaders have come together to promote a variety of activities, including nationally publicized academic seminars and a major annual convention, *La Semana Dominicana* (The Dominican Week),[10] which is held in major U.S. cities with large Dominican communities.

In Mexico, the pattern is more complicated. U.S. immigration policies, Mexican government responses to them, and the discrimination that emigrants experience are at the center of national news. However, respondents indicated that in Mexico, unlike El Salvador and the Dominican Republic, there is no widespread, institutionalized interest in emigrants. Mexican intellectuals and researchers, business groups, and NGOs do not autonomously produce, consume, or disseminate information about emigrants on a regular basis. Mexican society gobbles up a regular diet of news on emigration as an issue in U.S.–Mexico relations even as it pays little attention to emigrants and their relationship to Mexico per se.

In Guatemala and Colombia, emigrants receive little attention. Guatemalan respondents explained that this was because the nation had been long preoccupied with the civil war and was now engaged in the complicated process of restructuring its civil society. Moreover, one respondent suggested that the emigrants in Mexico have a greater saliency than those in the United States. Nonetheless, television has given some coverage to Guatemalan emigrants in the United States. To the extent that emigrants draw national attention in Colombia, it is likely to focus on those in Venezuela, who greatly outnumber those in the United States. But the nation has paid relatively little attention to emigrants overall because it, too, has been confronting violence at the hands of guerrillas and drug cartels for almost two decades. "How can we be involved with such an exotic issue when we have been living in Lebanon?" asked an NGO official.

Home Country Images of Emigrants

El Salvador

Salvadoran respondents described their emigrants in overwhelmingly positive terms, a universality of sentiment that may be explained by several factors. First, the emigrants left for good reasons: political conflict and lack of economic opportunities. Second, as one interviewee put it, "every family has a relative in the United States, and no one would like it if their relatives or close friends were disparaged." Third, as remittances grew and became a major source of sustenance for families, the government, and the economy, emigrants were transformed into "social heroes"—especially in rural areas, where they became role models because of their social mobility. Several respondents also asserted that without the remittances the country would have collapsed during the war. Thus, the country seems to share the sentiments voiced by a federal legislator: "El Salvador can only be grateful to its emigrant compatriots." Cognizant of these sentiments and the political capital to be earned from acknowledging emigrant contributions, the current government commissioned a major monument honoring *el hermano ausente* (the distant brother)[11] that is located at a major entrance to the capital city. In casual conversations about emigrants, Salvadorans from all ranks of society refer to this monument as a symbol of the nation's attitude toward emigrants.

The only negative aspect of the emigrants' image reflects the recent rise of *maras* (young gangs usually known as *gangas* in U.S. Hispanic slang). Established by repatriated Salvadorans, these gangs grow by recruiting local youth and resemble their U.S. counterparts in the use of distinctive clothing, "tagging," and wanton violence. According to several respondents, the *maras'* influence is greatest in rural areas, but at night they also "control" significant portions of central San Salvador. Their overall impact on Salvadoran society and on the image of emigrants is probably dampened by El Salvador's recent violent history and the high levels of crime that are its legacy.[12] In other words, the problems created by the *maras* have not been distinctive enough to generate an anti-emigrant backlash.[13]

It is noteworthy that Salvadoran images are based primarily on one aspect of the emigrant experience. That is, emigrants are depicted in terms of their economic success and their contributions to the Salvadoran economy. Our respondents made no reference to how emigrants are evolving in the United States and contributing to American cultural life.

Dominican Republic

Dominican society also has very positive but more diverse and balanced images of its emigrants, in part because it has a greater variety of institutions with links to Dominican groups in the United States and in part because of the rising political power of Dominican emigrants in New York City.[14] Respondents described emigrants in terms of the contributions they are making to U.S. literature, music, politics, and the academy. They also referred to the opportunities emigrants have created for themselves as entrepreneurs specializing in limousine services and *bodegas* (traditional neighborhood groceries).[15] This overwhelmingly positive portrait is reinforced by the persona of the current national president, a vigorous, articulate, and charismatic man who was born in the Dominican Republic but raised and educated in the United States. To many, he embodies the emigrant.

Nonetheless, a negative aspect of the emigrant's image developed in the 1980s. Thanks to television and some emigrants and returnees, a stereotype of emigrants as drug traffickers and criminals emerged. These stereotypical "bad guys" were depicted as living in New York City and wearing heavy gold necklaces;[16] society nicknamed them *los cadenudos* (the guys with the big chains) and "Dominicanyorks" (Guarnizo 1994). Indeed, the market for such necklaces became so substantial that, according to one respondent, it created an economic niche for Dominican jewelers. This image grew so rapidly that civic leaders mobilized to create an alternative image that would highlight the positive roles of emigrants in the United States and the Dominican Republic. Their effort contributed to the institutionalization of *La Semana Dominicana*, as described above.

Mexico

Mexico has complicated and contradictory images of its emigrants (de la Garza 1980). Government and the press are the only institutions that regularly generate information about emigrants, and both emphasize very limited aspects of the emigrant experience. Several respondents—including a senior official of the Ministry of Foreign Relations, a presidential adviser on emigration, and a distinguished journalist—noted that these sources almost always depict emigrants as loyal Mexicans whose economic needs make them vulnerable to American greed and racism. The dominant image emerges from stories on festivals celebrating Mexican national holidays in the United States, on remittances that indicate how loyal emigrants are to their nation, and on discriminatory and violent episodes in which emigrants are victimized. A scholar who advises Mexican officials on migrant issues noted that, "There is little discussion of emigrant resentments toward Mexico, or of the extent to which some Mexican villages are dependent on remittances, or of the successes achieved by many Mexican emigrants, or of the extent to which second- and third-generation Mexican Americans incorporate into American society."

One respondent cited two recent cases, the exploitation of deaf-mute undocumented immigrants in New York and the execution of convicted murderer Irineo Tristán Montoya in Texas,[17] to illustrate how emigrants are portrayed in Mexico. The New York case was originally portrayed, he said, as "an example of how the United States enslaves Mexicans. When it was learned that the people running the ring were Mexicans, coverage dropped. Intellectuals didn't engage the issue; there were no editorials, no sense of collective shame." Similarly, "coverage of Irineo Tristán Montoya never focused on his crime, on the people killed. Instead, he was portrayed as an example of how Americans discriminate against Mexicans and became a hero."[18]

These images suggest that Mexican government and society are less interested in emigrants per se than in how their maltreatment in the United States can be used to justify and reinforce traditional anti-American attitudes. Indeed, emigrants have for decades been viewed with disdain in Mexico and derisively described as *pochos*—vulgar, lower-class Mexicans who have adopted some of the worst aspects of American culture. Respondents agreed that this attitude is much less prevalent today, but even government officials responsible for emigrant outreach acknowledged that such sentiments persist among officials and in society at large. An official of the *Academia Mexicana de Derechos Humanos* (Mexican Academy of Human Rights) suggested that this bias is rooted in the way Mexican elites view the lower classes: "They don't like these people when they are living in Mexico; why should they like them when they emigrate?" Another respondent noted that, with very few exceptions, the nation's elites still harbor the negative image of Mexicans in the United States developed by Octavio Paz in *Labyrinths of Solitude*. Their attitude is exemplified by a comment made in 1996 to a member of our research team by a senior member of the Salinas de Gortari administration (1988–1994): "Respectable people don't emigrate" ("*La gente decente no emigra*"). A 1997 poll in Mexico City conducted by *Reforma,* a leading newspaper, indicates that the city's society at large shares these views. When asked, "What is your opinion of Mexicans who go to work in the United States?" 47 percent of respondents said "very bad or bad," 27 percent said "very good or good," and 23 percent said "neither good nor bad."[19]

Colombia

Although emigrants are not an important issue to Colombian society,[20] our interviewees were able to categorize them into three groups, all viewed positively. The largest group includes the typical migrant who left the country in search of better economic opportunities. A smaller but very important group consists of professionals, especially doctors, who have enjoyed great success in the United States. A third group, and one that is unique to Colombia, consists of prisoners. Because of domestic politics, this group, although small, is probably the most visible. The Colombian Congress approved legislation requiring the Secretary of Foreign Relations, through its consulates in the United States, to maintain regular contact with these prisoners to ensure that their human and constitutional rights are respected. Several respondents suggested that this legislation was introduced by congressmen linked to drug cartels who wanted to signal that the cartels take care of their employees. The legislation passed because of nationalistic and humanitarian reasons. Opposition was also hobbled by the fact that a large number of prisoners, many of whom are women, have no previous criminal record and no real involvement in the drug trade. Instead, they are working-class Colombians with few economic options who agreed to a risky, one-time trip as "mules" in exchange for a substantial payoff.[21] One of our interviewees in New York noted: "They are not evil people. No, they are simply poor, and in general very desperate because of debts or pushed by another urgent need for cash—such as medical bills or bankruptcy. Actually . . . and this is something most people are not aware of in the United States, all those who are hired as 'mules' are decent people with no previous criminal records. I understand that drug lords advertise for and take only good people who are likely to pass through customs without problems." Consequently, most of the prisoners are viewed sympathetically by Colombians both in the home country and in the United States.

Guatemala

Guatemalans have nebulous impressions of their emigrants.[22] As one respondent noted, "Futbol and how players will be selected for the world soccer championship in France is more important than our emigrants." There are, nonetheless, two major views. The population in general sees emigrants positively, emphasizing the obstacles that those emigrants overcome to improve their lives. Landowners and the more affluent segments of society, on the other hand, are said to be indifferent or hostile toward migrants, who are disproportionately drawn from the poorer ranks of society, including uneducated Indians and mestizos (Melville and Melville 1991).

In general, Guatemalan society seems more interested in its conationals living in southern Mexico (Aguayo 1991), and in repatriation issues linked to this very large group of refugees, than in the smaller, more distant group of Guatemalan emigrants in the United States.[23] Quite revealing is an ambitious study, cosponsored by the Mexican and Guatemalan governments, concerning binational relations (Monteforte Toledo 1997, 175–199). The chapter on migration details how northern Guatemala has become a decisive relay-station for Central American migrants seeking to move into the United States through Mexico. It also explains carefully how Guatemalan and Mexican authorities are trying to curb the flow of undocumented immigrants from other Central and South American nations. But it refers only briefly to the rising flow of Guatemalans who are also embarking on the long journey toward the United States.[24] This attitude is puzzling, and it seems to suggest that Guatemalan authorities have difficulty acknowledging that their country is now deeply embedded in a transnational network of migration, remittances, and official international relations that will become increasingly significant for national economics and politics.

Emigrants' Impact on the Home Countries

Respondents evaluated how emigrants affect their nation's economic, sociocultural, and political life. Their responses ranged from describing emigrants as having no visible impact to suggesting that they exert an impact on all major aspects of society. Again, there is no consistent pattern across countries emerging from the responses.

El Salvador

Respondents expressed ambivalence about the economic impact of emigrants. There is no doubt that emigrants have contributed to economic development. Their investments, combined with remittance-driven consumption, helped fuel the economic boom of the early 1990s. An outstanding example of emigrant investments is a housing development that was designed for and successfully marketed on the basis of photographs the contractor showed to emigrants in Los Angeles. More commonly, remittances have boosted small business development and helped sustain the purchasing power of much of the nation.

Because their impact is so substantial, however, remittances have become a major concern to government officials and independent analysts (Siri and Abelardo Delgado 1995). Remittances now constitute such a large part of the nation's capital, it is argued, that they have distorted and weakened the economy and altered work and consumption patterns to the detriment of the nation's future. El Salvador, according to this analysis, suffers from "Dutch disease."[25] As with Holland when it became dependent on tulip exports, El Salvador's reliance on remittances is said to undercut other industries. Families receiving remittances are unwilling to work for wages that would allow exporters to sell their goods at competitive prices. In rural communities with high emigration, reducing the willingness of individuals to join the labor market also changes the community's lifestyle. Additionally, the continuous expansion of the supply of dollars with no increase in the productivity of labor creates intense inflationary pressures that increase the costs of production for both domestic and export-oriented industries. According to one of our interviewees in San Salvador, the "Dutch disease model" predicts that the consequences of booming remittances will include a contraction of El Salvador's nonbooming activities (a prediction well supported by the slow growth of this country's agro-exports in the 1990s) as well as a real appreciation of the exchange rate.[26]

The availability of dollars has also affected consumption and investment patterns. Thanks in part to returning emigrants, Salvadorans are increasingly part of the "global market." That is, they want to use their dollars to purchase consumer items such as those that their returning kin bring with them or that they see on television. Poor families can now purchase items on credit, confident that their remittances will enable them to make their payments. Indeed, sometimes the emigrants make these purchases from Los Angeles or Washington,

D.C., in response to ad campaigns run by merchants in El Salvador. As a result, investors use their funds for consumption-oriented projects such as malls and stylish restaurants that yield quick returns rather than investing in industrial projects that may be riskier, require more funds, and take longer to yield profits.

The political impact of emigrants has changed in recent years. During the civil war, emigrants played a major role in mobilizing American opposition to the Salvadorean military by drawing attention to events such as the killing of Archbishop Oscar Romero and Jesuits at the University of El Salvador. Now their influence is more immediate. For example, one return migrant has been elected a provincial governor. Emigrants have also influenced relations with the United States by focusing public attention on the discrimination they experience there and on U.S. efforts to repatriate them. Their influence prompted the creation of an ad hoc, government-led multiparty delegation that traveled to Washington, D.C., to dissuade American officials from repatriating Salvadoran emigrants. Emigrant issues have even affected the ways congressional candidates campaign. One respondent remarked: "After I finished my stump speech, instead of being asked about local issues I was asked about Governor Pete Wilson and anti-immigrant attitudes in California and elsewhere. Imagine that—I had to know U.S. politics to be elected here! I was also told that if I really wanted to help the community, I should establish English classes to help future migrants prepare for their departure."

Emigrants make small financial contributions to the major political parties. That fact, combined with recognition of the importance of remittances, generated some discussion about the possibility of allowing emigrants to vote via absentee ballots. According to one respondent, officials in the leftist *Frente Farabundo Martí Para La Liberación Nacional* (Farabundo Marti National Liberation Front or FMLN) opposed the idea because they feared that emigrants would Americanize, become conservative, and support the right-wing *Alianza Republicana Nacionalista* (Nationalist Republican Alliance or ARENA). ARENA officials worried that emigrants would come under the influence of American liberals and turn to the FMLN. So the idea quickly died and currently has no champion.

Respondents also described emigrants' cultural impact. Remittances, as noted, have influenced consumption and work. *Maras* have exacerbated and altered criminal behavior. Emigrants and the social process of emigration have altered the identity of some villages to the extent that local streets are named in English. Overall, emigrants have been so influential that one analyst compared their impact to that of the Spanish conquest: "They are changing the food we eat, the language we speak, our religion and our economy. Nothing like this has occurred since the 16th century."

Dominican Republic

Many of these patterns are also evident in Dominican society. Although substantial, however, the overall effect there is much less obvious, perhaps because the relationship between emigrants and the home country is much more multifaceted. Economically, emigrants' major impact comes through remittances. An official of the *Banco Central* (Central Bank) estimates that the amount sent to an average family is $250 per month. These funds sustain poor families and help others establish or expand businesses such as car washes, repair shops, beauty parlors, and fast food restaurants. Additionally, emigrants have created a "remittance industry" that is expanding to include businesses and other institutions beyond the firms that actually transfer funds. The *Asociación de Remesedores* (Association of Money-Remitters), in collaboration with government officials, is developing a plan to enable emigrants to specify how the remittances they send to their families are to be spent. A sender could, for example, allocate $100 for groceries, $50 for tuition at a private school, $50 for rent, and the rest for use at the recipient's discretion.

Emigrants also affect the economy through direct investments, tourism, and the consumption of Dominican exports to the United States. According to the *Banco Central* official, in the 1980s the *Banco Hipotecario* (Mortgage Bank) had 80 percent of its loan portfolio with emigrants, although the figure has declined to 20 percent in recent years. As tourists, emigrants also contribute substantially to the home economy. As ethnic consumers in the United States, they serve as a market for Dominican agricultural exports. They thus create a niche through which Dominican exporters can penetrate the U.S. economy, a niche of such potential significance that a government task force is developing a plan to institutionalize this link.

Culturally, emigrants and return migrants have made themselves felt in several ways. Like the *maras* of El Salvador, some have exacerbated long-standing social problems, especially with regard to narcotraffic. Indeed, there is strong evidence that remittances are used as a cover for major money-laundering operations (see McFadden 1997). Some sections of the country are so linked to the United States that they take on American nicknames. The town of Sabana Iglesia, for example, is known as Sabana Church.

In general, emigrants have made a significant impact on traditional cultural practices, according to one respondent from the Dominican Republic. The *merengue*, the Dominican national dance, was losing ground to *salsa*[27] in the 1980s. Merengue musicians began migrating to New York City, where they found receptive audiences among Dominican émigré communities. As the stature of these communities increased, merengue's popularity in New York renewed its appeal in the Dominican Republic.[28] Today, merengue is again the nation's major dance form, just as it is the signature cultural statement of Dominican communities in the United States.[29]

Emigrants also play a major role in national politics (Guarnizo 1994). In 1982, thanks to fund-raising among the New York community, Jorge Blanco was able to become the presidential nominee of the *Partido Revolucionario Domicano* (Dominican Revolutionary Party, or PRD), and he went on to win the presidency. Since then, presidential candidates regularly campaign in U.S. cities with large Dominican populations. The PRD in particular has strong ties to emigrants, with offices in New York, Boston, Miami, and Philadelphia. A party official estimates that in 1996, 75 percent of its cash contributions came from emigrants. Yet while cash is important, political campaigns still depend much more heavily on in-kind contributions and volunteers.

Emigrants are permitted to vote in Dominican elections, but to do so they must return to their homeland and cast their vote on the day of the election. Few do so. In 1996, emigrants cast approximately one percent of all votes. Dominican leaders, appreciating how much emigrants contribute to the nation, raised two proposals to increase emigrant political involvement. The PRD has proposed allowing emigrant communities to elect a representative to the national congress. Furthermore, all political parties have publicly endorsed establishing absentee ballots for the emigrant community. Privately, however, party leaders viewed the latter proposal cautiously or opposed it. One analyst suggested limiting absentee balloting to local or congressional elections. Finally, the proposal to allow emigrants to vote by absentee ballot was approved in early 1998.

Mexico

Ironically, given the importance of immigration in U.S.–Mexico relations, the consensus among our respondents was that the impact of emigrants on Mexican society is not felt in Mexico City. To a substantial degree, Mexico City is a world apart from the rest of the country. As important as emigrants may be to the rest of the nation, they do not explicitly influence the cultural, intellectual, economic, or political life of the national capital. And because developments in Mexico City reverberate countrywide, shaping regional affairs as well as the national agenda, emigrants have less of an overall impact on national life than would otherwise be expected.

Emigrant issues are not without some impact of course. For example, the *Centro de Estudios Migratorios* (Center for Migrant Studies, or CEM), a fledgling institute at the *Universidad Nacional Autónoma de México* (Mexican National Autonomous University, or UNAM), puts such issues on its regular agenda. In general, however, Mexico's major research institutions do not systematically address emigrant issues, as do their counterparts in El Salvador and the Dominican

Republic. On the other hand, political parties, especially the governing *Partido Revolucionario Institucional* (Institutional Revolutionary Party, or PRI) and the center-left opposition *Partido de la Revolución Democrática* (Party of the Democratic Revolution, or PRD), are increasingly attentive to emigrant issues. According to one respondent: "All the states have emigrants, and they all benefit from remittances. Also, now, you get votes defending them because they have families here. So, the parties develop campaigns based on emigration." The parties are also institutionalizing campaigning among émigrés.

Nonetheless, one interviewee, who has advised governmental elites on emigrant issues, questioned the extent to which emigrants influence national politics. "The emigrant is very important in the national political discourse, but it is just rhetoric. The institution that has done the most and the one that is attacked for not doing enough is the government. But what have the unions done? Nothing. What have campesinos done? Nothing. The Governor of Zacatecas [a major emigrant sending state]? Nothing. University groups? Nothing. But they all 'support' the emigrants."[30]

On the other hand, the Mexican government recently approved dual nationality for all emigrants and absentee voting for those outside Mexico during elections.[31] Interviewees noted that these measures have not generated the kind of debate that occurred in El Salvador and the Dominican Republic over how such measures might affect the nation (e.g., do Mexican emigrants share Mexican values? Should they be allowed to determine close elections?) Instead, the issue is being addressed from a purely partisan perspective (which party will benefit most?)

Emigrants appear to exert somewhat more impact in Guadalajara than in Mexico City. Various governmental and nongovernmental institutions work with Mexican and Mexican American organizations and have well-institutionalized links with emigrant communities. Nonetheless, even though Jalisco is a major sending state, respondents and our observations do not indicate a highly visible, systematic impact on state or local affairs.

Colombia

Colombian governmental and nongovernmental institutions do not systematically engage issues affecting emigrants in the United States. The only exception is the legislative action regarding Colombian prisoners in the United States, as discussed above.

Guatemala

Emigrant remittances have significant positive effects on the Guatemalan economy, but the direct effects are more regional than national. One respondent said: "Before, all the peasant houses were made of natural materials (adobe, twigs), but now you see brick houses with tin roofs. Two towns have water pumps, and you see many bicycles and even used trucks and motorcycles. This is new, but very localized." Respondents also noted that emigrants have affected social and cultural life more generally. Emigrants have introduced many Guatemalans to international ways of doing business and standards of consumption. By reducing poverty, their remittances have helped reduce crime, which has been a major national problem. One respondent suggested that in the long term, emigrants' impact will be significant because they have introduced the "culture of migration" into a society where it had not existed before: "Young Guatemalans have begun thinking about a future abroad as an attractive and viable option." On the other hand, respondents agreed that emigrants have made no impact on the nation's political life.

Governmental and Nongovernmental
Relations with Emigrants

Latin American NGO Relations with U.S. Latino Organizations

In line with worldwide trends over the past twenty years, the NGO sector in Latin America has emerged as an important agent in civic and political life (Salamon 1994).[32] In several countries, NGOs have played a critical role in the move toward greater democracy (Bebbington and Thiele 1993). Most Latin American NGOs have received administrative advice and financial support from entities—usually other NGOs—outside their home countries, links that proved decisive in ensuring their survival in the hostile, authoritarian political environments characteristic of the 1970s and 1980s (Carroll 1987, Edwards and Hulme 1992). Not surprisingly, then, most of our interviewees indicated that their organizations maintained regular contact with foreign—predominantly U.S. and European—NGOs. However, though virtually all respondents indicated an interest in working with U.S. Latinos, almost none had done so to any significant degree. Contacts with Latino NGOs in the United States tend to be sporadic and are rarely followed up. This is particularly true with respect to Guatemalan and Colombian NGOs. On the other hand, major national Mexican, Dominican, and Salvadoran NGOs have slowly begun to reach out to their U.S. Latino counterparts over the past decade.

Most respondents who reported relationships with U.S.-based NGOs described their interaction as "functionally" rather than "ethnically" oriented. Women's groups, for example, tend to work with women's groups rather than with Latina organizations. And when cross-national Latino ties *are* established, they tend to follow national lines. For example, Dominican businessmen are linked to Dominican business associations in New York rather than to Puerto Rican or

Cuban organizations. A few respondents from various countries did indicate that they had contacted or worked with the National Council of La Raza (NCLR), a prominent "pan-Latino" organization that advocates for all Latinos living in the United States. Such relationships are, however, the exception according to our interviews with Latin American NGOs.

The strength and nature of established relations vary from country to country. A wide range of Dominican institutions regularly interact regarding a wide range of issues. In El Salvador, there appear to be only two types of institutionalized relations: those involving businesses dealing with remittances and those involving gangs. In Mexico, the strongest ties are between governmental agencies and emigrant communities, but some forms of connection at the strictly NGO level are also significant. For example, the Fundación Solidaridad Mexicano Americana (*Mexican American Solidarity Foundation*), a quasi-governmental institution that evolved out of governmental initiatives, may have a long-term impact. Established to foster relations with the Mexican-origin population of the United States, it includes prominent Mexicans and leaders of major U.S. Latino organizations. Other Mexican NGOs (such as human rights groups) are aware of ethnic organizations in the United States and tentatively plan to contact them in the future.

On the other hand, the president of the Mexican American Chamber of Commerce (MACC) indicated that establishing ethnic linkages would run counter to that organization's objectives: "The chamber is about promoting business relations and it would be counterproductive to select out businesses based on their ethnicity rather than on their productive capacity."[33] The chamber does work with Latino members of Congress, but with an eye to their role in promoting trade, rather than their ethnicity. However, the chamber's members are acutely aware of the need to increase the number of smaller firms that benefit from NAFTA. "Otherwise, it will fail," one leader predicted. The chamber has therefore instituted a "Partners in Progress" pilot program in Chicago that will attempt to increase the number of NAFTA beneficiaries by matching small firms with large ones. The program will not target Latino firms, mainly because doing so would "slow the process." However, given Chicago's large Hispanic population, the program is likely to boost the number of Latino businesses.

Colombian and Guatemalan NGOs seem to be the least interested in developing relations with similar conational organizations in the United States. Colombian NGOs simply do not perceive Colombian American NGOs as significant partners and would rather orient any outreach toward non-Latino and international nongovernmental organizations, with whom they already have long-standing connections. Guatemalan NGOs, whose representatives sometimes expressed a very weak interest, do not have any experience in this particular type of outreach and did not seem eager to develop it anytime soon.

Latin American Governmental Outreach
to U.S. Latino Organizations

Except for Guatemala, all the nations covered by our study have considered establishing or already have well-established outreach to their nationals in the United States. Colombia's efforts are limited to the absentee ballot. Colombian officials have discussed trying to mobilize emigrant organizations to oppose U.S. drug certification policies—a tactic that, according to a senior Colombian diplomat, U.S. embassy officials have also recommended. Nonetheless, no such effort has yet been developed.

Salvadoran officials are in the process of institutionalizing links with emigrant communities. Indeed, doing so is one of three major priorities of the Ministry of Foreign Relations. Influenced by Mexico's program, the ministry is designing various programs to assist emigrants, such as literacy classes that can be taught from El Salvador using distance learning technology. The Salvadoran Embassy in the United States has added the position of *Consejero Comunitario* (Counselor for the Community), whose responsibilities include meeting with organized emigrant groups, helping emigrants organize, helping groups send money for specific community development projects, and teaching emigrants their rights in the United States. A previous ambassador worked closely with emigrants in Washington, D.C., and helped stimulate interest in this relationship.

Salvadoran officials and emigrant leaders have used these links to create a united front opposing the proposed repatriation of emigrants who entered the United States under temporary status. Their joint effort began in 1996 when a bipartisan Salvadoran delegation traveled to Washington to discuss the matter with members of the U.S. Congress. Now, whenever the Salvadoran national president and other senior officials travel to Washington, meetings with community leaders form a central part of their agenda. It is noteworthy that U.S. officials in El Salvador have suggested that Salvadoran leaders work with emigrant communities on this issue.

Dominican officials too have developed close ties to emigrants. President Leonel Fernández Reyna has made it a priority, and the foreign ministry has responded by hiring emigrants to staff consulates and offices promoting exports and tourism. As a result, according to one official, these offices have grown in professionalism. Dominican officials have also begun working with business leaders to mobilize emigrants around key issues. For instance, arguing that Dominican exports have suffered greatly because of NAFTA, they have set out to persuade the U.S. Congress to pass legislation that would provide parity between Mexican and Dominican exports. The Dominican ambassador to the United States met with emigrant leaders in Washington and asked them to contact Congress about this issue. President Fernández Reyna has also exhorted emigrants to become U.S.

citizens so they can vote. According to a business leader, this would yield long-term benefits: "We could then identify the groups to develop a lobby. The problem now, however, is that while the nation's leadership understands the importance of parity legislation, the people (emigrants) do not." Officials have been encouraged in their efforts by Dominican politicos in the United States who point out that an increased Dominican vote may eventually help elect a conational to Congress who can then defend the interests of the Dominican Republic.

The Mexican government's emigrant outreach efforts are both deep and broad. Established during the Salinas de Gortari regime, they have grown under President Ernesto Zedillo's current administration. Among them are the *Paisano* program and the *Programa para las Comunidades Mexicanas en el Extranjero* (Program for Mexican Communities Living Abroad) (de la Garza 1997a). The former attempts to improve the treatment that returning migrants receive at the hands of Mexican officials by reducing corruption and abuse. The latter provides a wide range of services to Mexicans residing in the United States—including health, education, legal, and social services—and also helps them channel remittances toward local development in their communities of origin. Consuls have also helped arrange meetings between community leaders and visiting government representatives from Mexico. Moreover, many state and local officials from emigrant-sending cities and states meet with and provide services to emigrant groups.

Mexican officials have recently established close ties with virtually every noteworthy Mexican American organization. They began to reach out during the NAFTA debates, when the Mexican government systematically recruited support from Mexican Americans (Velasco 1997). Some were hired as lobbyists to mobilize such support; others arranged meetings between senior Mexican officials and Mexican American community leaders. Additionally, as part of its outreach, the Mexican government has begun bestowing the *Aguila Azteca* (Aztec Eagle), the highest recognition it may award a noncitizen, to distinguished Mexican Americans such as Raul Yzaguirre, president of NCLR, and Américo Paredes, professor emeritus of the University of Texas at Austin. In 1994 and 1997, the Mexican government invited large numbers of Mexican American politicos, media representatives, and academics to "observe" elections in Mexico.

Like their Salvadoran counterparts, Mexican officials now meet with Mexican American leaders when they visit the United States. Indeed, senior officials regularly attend the meetings of leading Mexican American and Hispanic organizations and use the occasions to deliver major addresses. For example, Secretary of the Treasury (formerly Secretary of Foreign Relations) José Angel Gurría attended the 1996 meeting of the National Association of Latino Elected and Appointed Officials (NALEO), while President Zedillo attended the 1997 annual meeting of the NCLR.[34] Two of our respondents suggested that Zedillo's speech there signaled a major change in the government's perception of Mexicans residing in the United States. As one of our interviewees said, Zedillo emphasized "what Latinos had accomplished on their own and spoke of them as another voice for Latin America, a voice that inspires and influences Latin America. Previously he would have said, 'How nice it is that you have maintained Spanish and Mexican customs.' "

Although their approaches vary, the governments of all five countries in our study have attempted to forge closer relationships with their emigrants in recent years (figure 3.2). This is true even of Guatemala's government, whose outreach remains the most limited.

Differences in Consular Policy Implementation at the City Level

Our interviews with consular and embassy officials in six major U.S. cities (table 3.11) revealed that governmental outreach to emigrant communities varies from city to city. We surmise that the variation stems not only from different

Figure 3.2: Changes in Latin American Consular Outreach Efforts toward Their Respective Diasporas in the U.S., 1985–1995

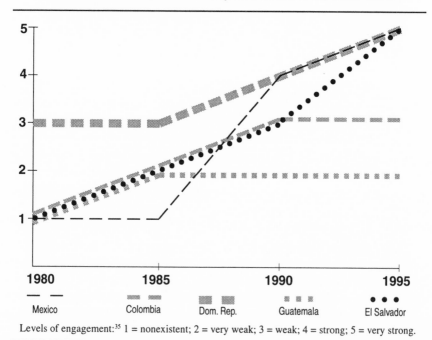

Mexico   Colombia   Dom. Rep.   Guatemala   El Salvador

Levels of engagement:[35] 1 = nonexistent; 2 = very weak; 3 = weak; 4 = strong; 5 = very strong.

Table 3.11 Assessment of City-Level Consular Outreach and Links with Local Diasporas[a]

Levels of interest and engagement	Non-existent	Very weak	Weak	Strong	Very strong
Country/Cities					
Mexico					
Los Angeles					✔
Chicago				✔	
Houston			✔		
New York			✔		
Washington, D.C.		✔			
Miami	✔				
Colombia					
Los Angeles					✔
Chicago				✔	
Houston			✔		
New York			✔		
Washington, D.C.		✔			
Miami			✔		
Dominican Republic					
Los Angeles[b]	–	–	–	–	–
Chicago			✔		
Houston		✔			
New York					✔
Washington, D.C.			✔		
Miami			✔		
El Salvador					
Los Angeles					✔
Chicago				✔	
Houston			✔		
New York			✔		
Washington, D.C.		✔			
Miami			✔		
Guatemala					
Los Angeles					✔
Chicago				✔	
Houston			✔		
New York			✔		
Washington, D.C.		✔			
Miami				✔	

[a] Based on interviews with consular officials and representatives of local Latino NGOs.

[b] Dominican Republic has no consular office in this city (1997).

local consular approaches, but also from the effects of varied urban environments as structured by politics, economics, and culture (DeSipio 1996). Table 3.11 and figure 3.2, summarize our findings regarding the intensity of local consular outreach efforts toward emigrant communities in Los Angeles, Chicago, Houston, New York City, Washington, D.C., and Miami.

Los Angeles

Los Angeles boasts a dynamic Latino business community and numerous Latino NGOs. It has been at the epicenter of recent political campaigns and legislative initiatives targeting the immigrant community. Moreover, Los Angeles is home to more people of Mexican and Salvadoran origin than any other city in the United States. Thus it should not be surprising that the Mexican and Salvadoran consulates have been prominent in city affairs. The Mexican consulate (González Gutiérrez 1993), for instance, has undertaken highly visible efforts to defend Mexican immigrants in Los Angeles, a move perceived by some as foreign intervention in U.S. affairs. Our interviews suggest that Mexican and El Salvadoran officials pay close attention to political events in Los Angeles because of the economic importance of their respective immigrant communities in that city.

Chicago

Hispanics (especially Mexicans and Puerto Ricans) maintain an important presence in city affairs. However, because there seems to be relatively little hostility among local authorities toward Latinos, consular officials do not feel compelled either to openly defend their conationals or to pursue aggressive outreach strategies. This is not to say that outreach does not take place. The Mexican consulate, for example, maintains a close relationship with umbrella organizations such as the Mexican American Legal Defense and Educational Fund (MALDEF) and the National Association of Latino Elected and Appointed Officials (NALEO) and has established a network incorporating at least sixty local Mexican immigrant organizations.

Houston

People of Mexican origin constitute the largest Latino group in Houston, but the Salvadoran and Guatemalan populations are substantial and growing rapidly. However, only the Mexican consulate has attempted to develop durable relationships with Mexican emigrants and Mexican Americans. As in other cities, the Guatemalan consulate has not pursued official government outreach efforts or undertaken local initiatives to develop a relationship with Guatemalan immigrant organizations. The Salvadoran consulate has also failed to develop links with its immigrant community in Houston, although the Salvadoran consulate-immigrant relationship in other cities, particularly Los Angeles, is strong. We are not sure of the reason, although the relatively small staff size of the Salvadoran consulate may partly explain it.

New York City

Colombian and Dominican consular officials have developed strong links in recent years with their conationals in New York. The Guatemalan, Mexican, and Salvadoran consulates continue to maintain weak or marginal links. This is particularly surprising with respect to Mexico, since the number of Mexicans in New York has grown rapidly during the past decade. The explanation may lie in the fact that Mexican emigrants come predominantly from indigenous areas of the country, which may create an "ethnic gap" between consular officials and the emigrant population. One of our interviewees in New York who works in close contact with Mexican immigrants told us that he had often heard them complain about lack of support from the city's Mexican consulate. According to our respondent, Mexican immigrants usually indicated that the local Mexican consulate treated them *"como extranjeros que apenas hablan bien el español"* ("like foreigners who can barely speak Spanish"). This impression is consistent with the results of other studies concerning Mexican immigrants in New York (Smith 1996). As we ourselves observed, a high percentage of Mexican immigrants in New York speak mostly indigenous languages, primarily Mixteco, and use Spanish (if they know it at all) only as a second language.[36]

Washington, D.C.

Only the Salvadoran consulate has attempted to forge a relationship with its emigrant community in Washington, probably because only the Salvadoran emigrant population constitutes a significant presence there. The prominent role of Salvadoran consular officials in Washington was demonstrated in November 1996, when a delegation representing two major Salvadoran political parties—FMLN and ARENA—met with U.S. and Salvadoran officials to discuss immigration. Notably, Salvadoran American leaders also attended the meeting. A Salvadoran NGO representative whom we interviewed in Washington articulated the event's significance: "For the first time since Salvadorans in the U.S. became a visible community, both U.S. and El Salvador official circles fully acknowledged our existence and foresaw the present and future potential role that we may—and most probably will—play in influencing relations between our ancestral and our host country. I truly believe it was the dawning of a new era."

Miami

As the unofficial "capital" of Latin America, Miami has nurtured vibrant Latin American emigrant communities. While Cuban Americans predominate, several nationality groups shape the city's political and cultural atmosphere and help foster ties between Miami and Latin American countries. Still, emigrant groups from our study countries do not constitute a significant presence in Miami. Only among Colombians and Mexicans do local populations exceed 50,000. Nonetheless, the Guatemalan consulate appears to have developed a surprisingly lively and cordial relationship with Miami's Guatemalan emigrants. Links were first developed seventeen years ago with the collaboration of the Guatemalan Chamber of Commerce (now the Central American Chamber of Commerce). This relationship seems to have been facilitated by the fact that most owners of small and mid-size businesses are White or Mestizo and of a middle-class background, traits shared with Guatemalan consular officials. Importantly, nearly 70 percent of trade between the United States and Guatemala flows through Miami, and in 1994 Guatemala ranked seventh in terms of imports and ninth in terms of exports among the city's leading trade partners (Jones-Correa 1995). Hence Miami remains a focal point in the United States for the Guatemalan government.

U.S. Latino NGOs: The View toward Latin America

In this section we will address two sets of questions. The first pertains to relations between U.S. Latino organizations and NGOs in Latin America: Do links exist between Latino organizations in the United States and Latin American NGOs? If so, how strong and enduring are they? The second deals with foreign policymaking in the United States: In what ways are U.S. Latino organizations involved in foreign policymaking? Are Latino organizations able to influence policy decisions? If so, which actors are influential? In addition, we try to determine whether U.S. Latino organizations' attitudes about Latin America encompass a broad U.S. Latino identity or instead have a more specific identity based mainly in their country of origin. In attempting to answer these questions we interviewed forty-nine leaders of Latino NGOs based in the United States (table 3.11).

With respect to the first set of questions, we have found relationships between Latino NGOs and Latin America to be relatively few and recent. With respect to the second set, we have found Latino NGOs to be involved little, if at all, in foreign policy issues and, except for two or three organizations, to exert almost no influence on U.S. foreign policy. We have also found that country-specific identification prevails over the notion of an overarching Latin American identity.

Before discussing these findings in greater detail, we should note that our research revealed two broad categories of Latino NGOs in the United States. The first category, which we label pan-Latino, is composed of organizations that focus on multiple issues of broad scope and that claim to be inclusive of all Latino groups. Examples of pan-Latino organizations include the NCLR, the Latin American Chamber of Commerce (LACC), the Hispanic Council on International Relations (HCIR), and the U.S. Hispanic Chamber of Commerce (USHCC). Ten of the forty-nine Latino NGO interviews were conducted with representatives of pan-Latino organizations. The second category, which we call "country-specific," consists of organizations targeting specific national-origin Latino groups, most of which maintain a much narrower agenda (sometimes focusing on a single issue) than pan-Latino groups. Examples of country-specific organizations include the Association of Salvadorans in Florida (ASAFLOR), the Nicaraguan American Chamber of Commerce (NACC), and the Colombian American Service Association (CASA). We interviewed thirty-nine NGO representatives from this category.

Most U.S. Latino organizations are primarily concerned with domestic issues, such as civil and political rights, gender equality, elections, and the social and economic status of Latinos (or specific Latino groups) in the United States. So are Latino elites in general. Other organizations focus on community-level issues, such as job training and English as a second language classes. In general, pan-Latino organizations are large and prominent, have a national constituency, maintain offices in several major U.S. cities, and advance a national political agenda. Country-specific organizations, in contrast, tend to maintain a local or regional focus, in terms both of issues and of organizing. There are exceptions, however. The Salvadoran American Health Foundation (SAHF) is a country-specific group with a national orientation, for example, whereas LACC is a pan-Latino organization with an *international* orientation. A few groups deal with intermestic affairs, such as migration.

Pan-Latino NGOs and Latin America

Pan-Latino groups place great rhetorical importance on international and Latin American affairs. However, when pressed for concrete examples, most respondents described only intermittent and isolated contacts with counterparts in other countries. This is not to say that pan-Latino organizations feel no interest in international and/or Latin American issues. Quite often the interest is there, but they lack the resources and/or information necessary to follow through, as seems to be common with Hispanic NGOs (see Gallegos and O'Neill, 1991). For example, the executive director of the Mexican American National Association (MANA) said she recognized that women's issues "cut across borders" and that "the conditions of women in Mexico, El Salvador, or Nicaragua are directly linked to the condition of women in this country." However, she offered little concrete evidence that cross-border Latina organizing in the Americas is becoming significant. An official with the U.S. Hispanic Chamber of Commerce (USHCC) noted: "We have concerns over international issues. We have [taken] positions [on trade-related] issues such as avocados; we have written on fast track. [International] issues are of great importance to us." Local affiliates evidence much less involvement. Only four out of the fifteen Latino chambers of commerce we surveyed indicated they are building active, ongoing relationships with their counterparts in Latin America. This finding is highly revealing because our research indicates that chambers of commerce are at the forefront among Latino NGOs in establishing transnational relations with counterparts in Latin America. By way of a final example, the president of the NCLR said that "international issues are growing in relevance to our organization and we are making sure we study closely those issues that are of concern to Latinos: we can't separate domestic from international issues when we deal with a group like Latinos." Nonetheless, even large organizations like NCLR continue to attach much more importance to domestic issues than to international affairs. The Latino elites in our survey, similarly, were most concerned with the progress and well-being of the Hispanic community in the United States. Nearly nine in ten (87%) said U.S. Latinos should be most concerned with the well-being of the Hispanic community in the United States. Three in four (74%) also said that what happens to the Hispanic community in the United States is more important to them than the state of U.S. relations with Latin America.

Pan-Latino groups directed by native-born Hispanic elites are more likely to emphasize domestic concerns, despite the fact that their leaders typically have extensive professional experience abroad. Most pan-Latino NGO respondents had traveled to Latin America and other regions of the world to attend international meetings and conferences during the past five years. However, their involvement in international and Latin American affairs typically reflected personal rather than organizational agendas. Institutional relationships are weak and relatively recent.

Pan-Latino NGOs do not maintain relations with Latin American governments and seldom mobilize with respect to Latin American issues. A few—such as NCLR and USHCC—have established contacts with Latin

American governments, but their programs are either quite recent or relatively small. Not surprisingly, Mexico is the country where these relationships are most developed. Even there, however, concerns tend to focus on the status of Latino immigrants in the United States, an intermestic issue as important to Mexico as to the United States.

Very few pan-Latino or country-specific organizations appear to engage foreign policy debates. As a Latino congressman noted in an interview, U.S. Latinos have not lobbied senior U.S. government officials regarding Latin American issues. Lobbying is instead done primarily by Latin American–based groups with ties to the United States or international organizations. Interviews with U.S. State Department officials who work with the five study countries confirmed the congressman's observation. Indeed, several of these officials noted the absence of Latino lobbying with respect to Central America, as a senior State Department official noted:

> The characterization of civil society NGO groups that approaches us, being the United States Department of State (USDOS) or an Embassy, on behalf of those countries tend to be European or U.S. driven. Over time, you will see the more educated Central American migrants taking up those causes. But for the time being it's been U.S. people through powerful international NGOs like Amnesty International (AI) and the Washington Office on Latin America (WOLA)—you know, a big umbrella organization—who have done the lobbying.

There are a few exceptions. For example, U.S.-based Colombian organizations—such as the Colombian Association of Professionals (CAP)—have lobbied in favor of congressional certification of Colombia's official antidrug efforts.

Overall, the few groups that have tried to exert foreign policy influence have focused on three broad issues: relations with Mexico; immigration; and development, including trade and aid. NCLR, for example, has lobbied Congress and the White House to increase foreign aid to Latin America. Starting in the 1990s, it began to lobby with respect to trade, development, and remittances, and it helped create the Hispanic Council on International Relations (HCIR). The HCIR is perhaps one of the very few institutions that according to its own programmatic statements "tries to provide a forum to discuss foreign policy and see Latino perspective on international issues." Yet its scope remains small, as its functions are limited to organizing talks throughout the year. NCLR also helped create the Mexican American Solidarity Foundation. The USHCC has supported increased trade and investment in the region and is working to extend its involvement beyond Mexico. The Southwest Voter Registration Education Project (SVREP) has sent election observers to Mexico and Central America and has studied political conditions in these as well as in other Latin American countries. This group even has an Intermestic Affairs Research Office.

Country-Specific NGOs and Latin America

There are differences among country-specific Latino NGOs in the United States, differences that manifest themselves in the way resources are mobilized and agendas defined and in the perceived importance of international issues and links. Some are also more active than others in establishing relationships with Latin American counterparts.

Country-specific Latino groups that are nationally organized in the United States have established more relationships with the home country than have strictly local groups. An organization with a national scope such as the Salvadoran American Health Foundation is stronger, larger, and more influential with respect to home country issues than the strictly local Association of Salvadorans in Illinois (ASI). Leaders of the smaller organizations usually identify domestic community issues as more important or urgent than issues in the Latin American home country. Moreover, ability and interest in engaging with the Latin American countries are affected by financial and human resources, as well as by the emotional attachment NGO leaders have to the country of origin.

National Cases

Mexico

Older, more established Mexican organizations, typically funded and managed by native-born Mexican Americans, are distinguished by their predominant involvement in domestic U.S. issues. Their work has dealt with issues such as business development, welfare, health, education, equal opportunity, and access to the political system. More recent Mexican organizations, mainly established by foreign-born Mexicans living in the United States, have concentrated their work on issues like immigration and labor rights in the United States. Another kind of Mexican organization has recently emerged but has a much smaller presence—Mexican clubs (González Gutiérrez 1995). In these clubs, Mexican immigrants forge ties with their hometowns over issues such as religious festivities, reconstruction of churches, schools, and other local development projects.

None of these groups exerts substantial influence on the national political scene in Mexico. Moreover, their mobilization vis-à-vis Mexican issues has been largely restricted to two forms. The first form is circumstantial: organizations that mobilized over NAFTA did so primarily with respect to domestic issues (e.g., migration, benefits to U.S. businesses, job losses, increased trade ties) and only secondarily with respect to Mexican issues (e.g., its trade position, labor and environmental concerns), which were promoted mainly by non-Latino groups in the United States (Eisenstadt 1997, Velasco 1997). The president of the William C. Velasquez Institute, for example, said, "Our positions on NAFTA and other issues are based on our understanding of Latino well-being and not on Mexican priorities" (Gonzalez 1998). The second form of mobilization is hometown-oriented: Mexican national and state officials have typically initiated such binational contacts, by means either of consular offices or of visits by Mexican state delegations to migrant centers in the United States. These Mexican authorities increasingly facilitate the connection between local immigrant groups and their hometowns (González Gutiérrez 1997). The actual relationships typically involve only the lower echelons of Mexican society. Some state governments have, however, now begun trying to promote partnerships between local authorities and emigrants through hometown associations. As Mexico moves toward a more representative political system and a less centralized government, newer and more intense links between regional homelands and their emigrants in the United States are beginning to take shape. The cases of Guanajuato and Zacatecas are the most interesting ones in this respect. Both state's governments have taken steps to help emigrants participate in local and regional political affairs as well as economic development programs.

El Salvador

El Salvador's population in the United States has a higher percentage of foreign-born immigrants than any other Latin American country-of-origin group. It is also a much younger group (historically speaking) that has only recently begun to develop links with its home country. Although Salvadoran organizations in the United States have grown in number since the peace accords were signed in El Salvador in 1992, there are few Salvadoran or Salvadoran American organizations in the United States that work on Salvadoran issues. The strongest immigrant organization working on such issues is the Salvadoran American Health Foundation, which works on health issues by providing preventive care materials to health centers in rural El Salvador. ASANOVA, the recently founded National Salvadoran Association, has attempted to focus on Salvadoran issues that affect Salvadorans in the United States and in El Salvador. There are also regional country-oriented organizations, such as the Association of Salvadorans in Illinois, or the Central American Resource Center (CARECEN), which have tried to look to both sides of the border while giving preference to issues affecting Salvadorans in the United States. Other organizations are newer and have fewer resources but have expressed concern about Salvadoran affairs. As in the Mexican case, government has recently made some efforts to help Salvadoran groups link up with their hometowns.

Unlike the Mexican case, however, Salvadoran organizations have been active in establishing relationships with their home country at various levels. Furthermore, although their political influence in El Salvador has not been substantial, Salvadorans in the United States have established better connections with home country elites. This relatively strong relationship may reflect the Salvadorans' widespread recognition that remittances from their emigrants in the United States are helping keep the Salvadoran economy afloat.

Dominican Republic

Of the immigrant groups examined in this study, Dominicans are among the most engaged with home country affairs. They have mobilized in both the United States and the home country over issues that affect Dominicans in both countries (e.g., deportation of common criminals back to the Dominican Republic). Moreover, the relationships between Dominicans in the United States and their fellows in the Dominican Republic are stronger and better consolidated than those of El Salvador or Mexico. Remittances from migrants are not the only source of interest for island Dominicans; cultural exchange and political support have become significant as well. The relationship is reciprocal and, unlike those of the other two countries, it encompasses most sectors of society. In New York, Chicago, and Miami, Dominicans have actively pursued links with their home country and have also been contacted by groups in the Dominican Republic. Crucial issues in the bilateral relations between the Dominican Republic and the United States, such as migration, law enforcement, and trade, are of concern to Dominican communities and their leaders in the United States. Moreover, Dominican Republic representatives are trying to promote engagement with their emigrants in a nonpartisan fashion—that is, as an official governmental outreach and not as a tool for the Dominican political party (or parties) in power.

The demographic growth of Dominicans in New York, where most congregate, has bolstered their power in city affairs, which in turn has bolstered their influence on homeland Dominican issues. Probably one of the most important sources of their growing power has been their organizational skills, which one of our Dominican interviewees in New York associated with the contemporary (1940s– 1990s) Dominican exodus to the United States. According to our respondent, numerous intellectuals and politicians—including labor leaders, student activists, peasant organizers, and professionals with a well-developed political discourse—sought refuge from the Trujillo dictatorship in the 1950s, and the island's convulsive politics impelled further waves of political migrants into the United States in subsequent years. These migrants brought with them not only strong partisan convictions, but also organizational savvy and political experience.

However, the emergence of Dominican organizations in New York took time, and it was not until the early 1980s that they really became key players in citywide affairs. Four Dominican organizations in particular—the Community Association of Progressive Dominicans, the Northern Manhattan Coalition for Immigrants Rights, Alianza Dominicana, and Latinos United for Political Action—gained prestige and influence in New York City as they became deeply involved with local school board politics. Their growing clout helped elect several Dominican activists like Guillermo Linares (now a city councilman) and Apolinar Trinidad to School Board No. 6, in Washington Heights. In turn, the new elected officials of Dominican descent helped link Dominican NGOs in New York with their country of origin and encouraged them to participate in initiatives to aid the needy in the Dominican Republic.

Colombia

Colombian organizations in the United States exhibit a different kind of relationship and mobilization. Such organizations have provided in-kind assistance to local and national organizations in Colombia, supported that nation's certification by Congress as a valuable partner in the war on drugs, and helped raise interest in the dual citizenship initiative. Despite these efforts, the Colombian government has not shown a corresponding interest in Colombians in the United States. Although there is an acknowledgment that stronger relations are needed, there are no visible efforts to develop them.

It is also important to stress that although some U.S. Colombian organizations have a marked international orientation, the majority are domestically oriented. While paying considerable attention to national events in Colombia, these organizations mobilize primarily over domestic issues that affect their well-being: legalization, employment, and social services. The director of the Colombian American Service Association stressed this point clearly when he was interviewed in the fall of 1997:

> There are some organizations that send aid abroad [to Latin America]. We don't. We realize that the time and resources spent here will give us a better return in the long term than if we [direct them] to [the Colombians]. We help people improve their life here and in return somehow the person will help the organization.

In 1995 various Colombian organizations created a Political Action Committee named *Coalición Colombo Americana* (Coalition of Colombian Americans) to lobby Congress generally and the Hispanic Congressional Caucus in particular (CUPULA 1995, 5–6). This effort was independent of Colombian government efforts vis-à-vis decertification. We found no evidence of any political connection between Colombians in the United States and the Colombian government. On the other hand, we did learn that some Colombian trade offices (e.g., the one in Los Angeles) have tried to reach out to Colombians in the United States to lobby over trade issues.

Guatemala

Guatemalans have a smaller number of organizations and their activities are either markedly domestic or international; few engage in what we have called intermestic affairs. Organizations with an international orientation are not exclusively ethnically oriented, although most of their members are Guatemalans. Moreover, they have exercised no influence on domestic affairs or U.S. foreign policy. One exception is the Organization of Solidarity with Guatemala (OSGUA), which has experience in networking and mobilizing over Guatemalan human rights issues. Mobilizing its members through letters, phone calls, or direct meetings, this group has been active in writing to Congress and lobbying state representatives to make them aware of issues in Guatemala.

National versus Hemispheric Latino Identity

A recent study on Latino interest in Latin America showed that "rather than having homogenous views, differences in national origin, nativity, language competence, and racial self-identification produce variations in Hispanic perspectives on these issues" (de la Garza et al. 1997, 420). Our interviews with Latino elite organizations suggest the same pattern. Except for NCLR and some Hispanic chambers of commerce, organizations showed a predominantly country-specific identification. While pan-Latino ethnic identity was explicitly articulated as an important part of many organizational missions, when it came to international issues, country-specific identification prevailed over the notion of an overarching Latino identity. "Specific country-oriented and defined Latino identities are still more important than the transnational Latin identity," said one of the Latino academics we interviewed. The same interviewee concluded that

> the migration flows reinforce national attachments; these migrant families which come from the same country of origin have in many cases known each other for generations and transmit their Latin American nationalist values to their children beyond the second and even third generation. Interactions with other Latino migrant communities in the host country seem to develop very slowly and only in those cities or regions in which several groups of different Latin American origins have a significant demographic, political, and cultural presence.

Thus, Latin American identification reflects specific country of origin attachments rather than a regionwide commitment.

Conclusions

In this chapter we have examined old and new links between U.S. Latino groups and governmental as well as nongovernmental organizations in Colombia, the Dominican Republic, El Salvador, Guatemala, and Mexico. We have concentrated primarily on the ways in which Latino communities in the United States shape contemporary U.S.–Latin American relations.

There are, of course, many topics that an exploratory study such as this one cannot cover. For example, we have not examined certain small-scale phenomena such as binational households, transnational communities, and hometown associations of migrant origin, all of which are coming to prominence in the study of modern transnational processes. However, it is important to keep in mind that we have been concerned here mostly with the net effect that the emergence of U.S. Latinos as the nation's second-largest minority has on relations between the United States and their ancestral lands and on U.S. foreign policy. Thus, while we have not examined those small-scale phenomena per se, we have taken them into account when observing any "spillover" effect they may have on the so-called high politics that control hemispheric relations.

U.S.–Latin American Relations: General Patterns and Future Trends

Throughout this chapter we have described the demographic transformation of Latino communities in the United States during the 1980s, when Latinos became an increasingly diverse group with an increasingly visible economic and political presence. This transformation has coincided with the end of the Cold War and with an era of intense globalization. We have noted that cross-border relationships and hemispheric processes have been affected by the growth of the U.S. Latino population. We have also examined home country perceptions of emigrants, the impact of emigrants on the home countries, Latin American government efforts (or failure) to reach out to emigrant communities in the United States, and the extent to which U.S. Latino NGOs are domestically or internationally oriented.

Perhaps the most striking general conclusion to emerge from our research is that there is no broad and clear pattern of relations between Latinos and their countries of origin. National differences as well as differences between native and foreign-born Latinos remain prominent. According to our findings, it seems premature to try to make any generalization concerning Latino–Latin American relations beyond national specificities. Such a generalization can perhaps never be made unless the various Latino groups in the United States develop a more clearly defined common identity.

As long as *Latina/o* remains as an external label used by the society at large to describe a heterogeneous group without an internalized common identity, the different national Hispanic communities will continue to identify primarily by country of origin. Following this line of reasoning, it seems only logical to assume that as long as specific countries of origin remain a prominent marker of identity, the notion of *Latin America* will remain as abstract a category of social perception and action as is the term *Latino*. So far, only broad commonalties allow Mexicans, Colombians, Salvadorans, Dominicans, and Guatemalans to relate to one another as having some kind of shared identity. Based on this study, it seems to us that only Latino elites tend to claim some form of pan-Latino identity—and even they seem to do so more at a rhetorical level than at a practical one.

On the other hand, the trend toward greater hemispheric integration is very powerful. Economic globalization coupled with regional integration via free trade agreements has intensified exchanges of all kinds, not merely financial and commercial ones. New cultural, political, and ethnic hemispheric processes are emerging, fueled both by regional economic integration and by greater movements of people across national borders. Migratory flows—mostly bound from Latin America to the United States but also between Latin American countries—have also forged new links. While it may be premature to identify any well-established pattern of attitudes and practices at the level of hemispheric relations and policies, certain basic trends can be noted.

There has been a clear movement toward stronger links between our five study countries and the United States. Old links such as migration and remittances have reached a new plateau. Migration (a northward flow of labor) and remittances (a southward flow of money) are not novel processes (Nayyar 1994), but their effect upon the interweaving of domestic and international policies is nonetheless different. Today, migration and remittances clearly constitute the strongest "spontaneous" interactions between the United States and its neighbors to the south.

However, even in this respect, national differences remain significant. Mexico and Colombia interact with the United States regarding other issues that are more prominent (foreign trade in the case of Mexico; drug and money flows in the case of Colombia); relations with the Dominican Republic, Guatemala, and El Salvador are dominated by immigration-related issues such as remittances. In fact, El Salvador and the Dominican Republic have become so dependent upon these monies that one of our interviewees in Latin America sarcastically called them *remittance republics*, paraphrasing the old derogative label *banana republics*. Guatemala is moving rapidly in the same direction, but is far from establishing such a dependent relationship with the United States.

In fact, remittances have come to exemplify an intermestic process in which domestic and international phenomena mix in novel ways, affecting both the sending and the receiving countries. In terms of official policies and relations between the United States and Latin America, migration and remittances have had a clear spillover effect. The benefits that remittances bring to Latin American economies and households have no doubt created greater incentives for people to migrate—and for Latin American governments to encourage this process. However, migration in turn has generated anti-immigrant sentiment in U.S. states with many Latino immigrants.

Responding to domestic pressure, the U.S. government has attempted to reduce the flow of immigrants. This partially explains why some Latin American countries have made more comprehensive and intense outreach efforts toward emigrants in the United States. These countries perceive U.S. migration policies (which, oddly enough, have primarily taken the form of domestic measures) as a threat to their own domestic political and economic stability. Thus, we see two spontaneous transnational processes shaping and being shaped by domestic political forces and policies. Some may argue that emigrant outreach efforts are merely an extension of countries' official foreign policies. However, because these policies are not targeted at the U.S. government, they cannot, strictly speaking, be considered traditional international initiatives. Nor are outreach efforts truly oriented toward improving the status of Latino immigrants in the United States. Rather, they are oriented toward improving domestic economic and political conditions in Latin America, as well as toward garnering support for the incumbent regime.

U.S. Latinos and U.S.–Latin American Relations: Emerging Links

The debate over the NAFTA treaty marked a turning point in the role that U.S. Latinos play in official international relations with Latin America. For the first time Latino influentials in the United States were actively targeted by both a Latin American government (Mexico in this particular case) and the U.S. government. The governments were partners in the effort, which naturally facilitated greater Latino involvement. Latinos (mainly Mexican American leaders) reacted positively to the outreach and supported both governments in the political and media battle over NAFTA. Some scholars, such as Samuel Huntington (1996), have argued that this involvement illustrated the increased influence of so-called ethnic lobbies in defining and thus fragmenting U.S. foreign policy interests. Nonetheless, exactly the opposite argument can be made if one notes that Mexican American leaders were mainly supporting U.S. strategic interests and their own self-interest rather than promoting the Mexican government's political agenda.

Furthermore, examining the modern history of Western Hemispheric relations yields only isolated examples of Latinos supporting the interests of their home country in opposition to the United States. Probably one of the few instances was when Colombian elites in the United States lobbied for Colombia's certification. To be sure, U.S. Colombians were actively supporting their home country's government. Yet their goal may well have been to improve Colombia's international image so that their own status in the United States would not be further damaged by negative media coverage about their home country.

Since the passage of NAFTA, all Latin American countries with an important emigrant community residing in the United States have sought to improve relations with their émigrés and with the greater Latino community. Mexico has been at the fore of this effort. Moving from a traditional lack of interest in Mexican Americans and Mexicans in the United States, Mexico's government launched the ambitious Program for Mexican Communities Living Abroad. It is a cultural and political outreach program designed to reactivate links with the Mexican American community and to strengthen official links with Mexicans residing in the United States. Nonetheless, despite its ambitious design and costly budget, this program has yielded rather minor results. While it has probably contributed to a rapprochement between Mexico and Mexicans living in the United States, it has not clearly strengthened Mexico's governmental clout among Mexican migrants or Mexican Americans.

Like the other Latin American countries examined in this study, Mexico is undergoing a dramatic political transformation at home. Civil society plays an increasing role in shaping the country's political and socioeconomic life, and a series of new right- and left-wing political parties are competing now for both domestic and international support. Mexico's official outreach program may lack true legitimacy and credibility among its target community because of two additional factors. First, it is not easy to convince a formerly neglected community of the sincerity and depth of this sudden official interest. A long history of estrangement cannot be reversed in just a few years, and the cleavages that separate a working-class migrant population from the ancestral country's wealthy political elite cannot be easily overcome. Second, Mexico's official outreach is curtailed by the very nature of the policy, which simply has very little to offer Mexicans and Mexican Americans in terms of improving their life in the United States. Mexico's outreach efforts seek to strengthen links in ways that are clearly favorable to the country's governing elites; it is not clear how those efforts benefit the migrant population. Regardless of its obvious shortcomings, Mexico's official outreach policy remains a "showcase" and a model for the new official attitudes that are informing Latin America's official programs vis-à-vis U.S. Latinos. The Dominican and Salvadoran governments seem to be as eager and open as Mexico about their intentions to establish closer, better official relations with compatriots in the United States.

The U.S. Salvadoran community emerged in the 1980s as result of civil strife in the home country. Composed mostly of people who opposed the policies of the political forces governing El Salvador (then and now), they naturally tend to be skeptical toward any official policy of rapprochement. The most influential Salvadoran organizations in the United States were created as part of an institutional network of NGOs critical of U.S. policies in Central America and with the purpose of helping Salvadoran refugees to resettle in the United States. As El Salvador achieves domestic stability and democratic consolidation, relations between U.S. Salvadorans and their home country government are gradually improving. Here again we see some of the same factors that limit the effectiveness of Mexico's official outreach: lack of a clear proposal for how to help Salvadoran migrants in the United States improve their material and political conditions, and the emergence of competing political forces in El Salvador that are beginning to seek closer connections with Salvadorans in the United States.

There is one great difference in the relations that have been and are being established between Salvadorans in the United States and El Salvador. In contrast to Mexican society, Salvadoran society entertains very positive feelings toward its conationals living in the United States. U.S. Salvadorans are perceived almost as national heroes, and there is something akin to a national myth about what is considered their epic migration to the United States, their increasing presence in that country, and the crucial role their remittances play in assisting the domestic economy. This feeling is not being fueled by any official propaganda, but is a genuine feeling of admiration and respect for the "distant brothers and sisters." And it is not a trivial factor. In Mexico, where there is no such widespread positive attitude toward its emigrants, official outreach efforts lack the natural and spontaneous support of the home country populace (except perhaps at certain local and regional levels).

The importance of this natural and spontaneous warmth toward compatriots who have emigrated to the United States is best seen in the case of the Dominican Republic. The Dominican government has so far not developed any particular official initiative designed to strengthen links with Dominicans in the United States. Nonetheless, relations between Dominicans in the United States and their ancestral lands remain close and very dynamic, in great measure because of the predominantly positive and friendly attitudes on the part of the Dominican people with regard to their emigrants in the United States.

Colombia, a distant country of almost 36 million people, has neither at the popular nor at the government level developed an outreach program toward Colombians in the United States. A recent policy study by the *Universidad Nacional de Colombia* (National University of Colombia) on U.S.–Colombia binational relations dedicates only two pages—out of a total of ninety-five—to Colombian emigrants in the United States, and rather pessimistically concludes that "the negative image of Colombia that is persistently projected by U.S. media makes it very difficult for our emigrants to seek and establish political alliances, and to formulate claims that may be listened to by Washington D.C. As long as this negative perception persists, it will be unrealistic to expect that Colombian migrants can influence U.S. policy towards their country of origin, as has already been done by the Cuban, the Haitian, and the Dominican communities" (our translation from the Spanish original in IEPRI 1997, 70). One of the lessons we extract from this case is that when neither civil society nor official circles are interested in strengthening links, emigrants' efforts to build a closer and deeper relationship with the country of origin will not become significant.

Guatemala, on the other hand, is sending more and more migrants to the United States and these in return are remitting increasing amounts of money. Although Guatemalan authorities remain rather indifferent toward Guatemalans in the United States (a feeling that seems to be reciprocated), it can be surmised that these relations will tend to warm up—particularly with the end of the civil war in December 1996.

In sum, we observe no simple correlation between increased hemispheric integration—at the spontaneous and official levels—and the influence that Latinos may exert upon governmental binational policies. Hemispheric integration via free trade agreements and transnational phenomena such as migration and remittances are powerful trends. However, official international policies in the United States and Latin America remain beyond the direct influence of U.S. Latinos. There is no evidence to suggest that Latino "ethnic lobbies" are becoming prominent in shaping the U.S. foreign agenda or in influencing the international policies of their countries of origin. There is evidence, however, that Latinos may become crucial players in those few instances in which their participation is sought simultaneously by the United States and their country of origin. In such cases Latinos are being "called upon" rather than taking the initiative themselves. We see little impact or even interest on the part of U.S. Latinos in terms of influencing official binational or international relations. As we have already indicated, the "spillover effect" is felt mostly in either strictly domestic or intermestic political decisions and initiatives. Most U.S. Latino influence upon hemispheric relations is exerted spontaneously and in ways that can be best understood as oblique or indirect.

Before we began this research we had great expectations regarding the role of the "Third Sector" (NGOs) in shaping international policies and relations between the United States and Latin America. So much has been written and said about the emergence of the Third Sector that we truly expected to uncover evidence of its rising prominence. However, we found almost no evidence that either U.S. Latino NGOs or Latin American NGOs are engaging international relations or networking with one another across national borders in any significant way. Perhaps because they lack the necessary resources, connections, or knowledge, Latino and Latin American NGOs are not engaging each other nor addressing international issues in any way that may herald dramatic changes in the near future. They remain thoroughly committed to activities and issues that are strictly domestic—although their agendas may have some unintentional international consequences. U.S. Hispanic and Latin American chambers of commerce or trade offices seem to be the exception, and mainly in terms of strengthening links between business communities in the United States and Latin America.

U.S. Latinos are clearly much more engaged with domestic issues than with foreign policy. Nonetheless, because many of these issues are linked to international ones, Hispanics increasingly find themselves enmeshed with foreign policy. Moreover, even though they focus primarily on domestic problems, Latinos retain close cultural and economic ties to their home countries and Latin America generally. Thus, even though Latinos are not now systematically attempting to influence the nation's foreign policy, the growing convergence of domestic and foreign policy concerns combined with their strong bonds to Latin America suggest that Latinos are likely to play an increasingly important role in shaping the nation's international agenda.

This growing potential is why Latin American officials have initiated efforts to institutionalize their links to Hispanics. Not only are they interested in strengthening existing cultural and economic ties, but they also hope to have Latinos become an ethnic lobby that will support them in their dealings with the U.S. government. Latin American governments, in sum, hope to have Latinos play the same role in U.S.–Latin American relations that Irish, Turkish, and Jewish immigrants have played regarding U.S. policy toward Ireland, Turkey, and Israel.

There is no way to know precisely when U.S. Latinos will make international issues a political priority or what specific issues will top their agenda. What does seem clear is that they will bring their own views to bear on these issues with increasing frequency. Their perspectives will not be those of the home country or of mainstream America, but will instead reflect their experiences as immigrants who, in becoming Americans, are transformed into ethnic minorities. As "new" Americans, they are as unlikely to echo home country interests as they are to see Latin America through the same lens as the traditional foreign policy establishment. Rather, they may well be expected to propose new initiatives that challenge their home country governments, U.S. officials, or both. In other words, Latinos will join with other citizens to help shape the nation's priorities and define the national interest.

Notes

Numerous respondants referred to in this chapter chose to remain anonymous.

1. We would like to express our appreciation to Karen Escalante, Scott Graves, and Kristin Fossum for their editorial assistance with this chapter.

2. We chose these countries because they have the five largest immigrant communities in the United States. We purposely excluded Cuba and Cuban Americans because they are still enmeshed in the dynamics that characterized the Cold War.

3. Actually, according to our survey, Latino leaders are keenly aware of both the internal diversity of the U.S. Latino community and that of Latin American countries of origin. Moreover, about six in ten (58%) feel that the heterogeneity of backgrounds and identities among U.S. Latinos has weakened the community's domestic and international political clout.

4. This factor determined not only the Latino groups to be studied, but the U.S. cities in which domestic interviews were to be held.

5. We define "Latino elites/leaders" in this study very broadly to include any individual that may exert some level of collective influence—be it through politics, culture, nonprofit activities, intellectual endeavors, information or business—upon the U.S. Latino community.

6. Latin American interviews were conducted primarily with officials based in capital cities (the exception being Mexico, where we conducted several interviews in Guadalajara). Confining our interviews to capitals poses the danger that we will miss important dimensions of U.S.–Latin American relations developing in the provinces. However, given the degree to which economic, cultural, and political life in Latin America is concentrated in capital cities, we believe it is safe to assume that emigrant impacts on relations between the United States and the home countries are most likely to manifest themselves in these urban centers.

7. Those responding to the survey included Hispanics in academia (27%), business (21%), the media (18%), NGOs and nonprofits (14%), the public sector (10%), and others. Of the total, 61% had been born in the United States; 40 percent were of Mexican heritage; and 69 percent were male and 31 percent female. Their median age was forty-seven. The survey was fielded between September 28 and December 31, 1997.

8. For additional information on Colombian, Dominican, Guatemalan, and Salvadoran immigrants, see the Tomás Rivera Policy Institute/NALEO Educational Fund's series on emerging Latino populations by Louis DeSipio and Harry P. Pachon.

9. We use the word "diaspora" rather loosely to describe a community of migrant origin that retains a significant bond (be it a purely imaginary or a strong material and institutionalized system of links) with ancestral lands. For an in-depth discussion on this subject see Shain 1994 and 1995, Sheffer 1994, and Esman 1986.

10. According to its organizers, *La Semana Dominicana* is "a joint effort [by the Dominican community in the United States and the Dominican Republic] to take what is best of Dominican Republic and present it to the public at large . . . Dominican Week is composed of academic seminars on the history and culture of the Dominican Republic,

commercial gatherings designed to promote trade, exhibition of Dominican products and the presentation of Dominican artists" (Amiana 1993, 14).

11. It is difficult to translate this phrase accurately. When a public relations firm in El Salvador tried to back-translate the phrase "hermano ausente" into Spanish from the English "distant brother," people used the phrase "hermano distante." However, this phrase left many unhappy because it had a negative meaning. Therefore we use "distant brother," intending it to mean "the longed-for brother."

12. According to Michael Shifter, "El Salvador is now believed to be the world's most violent country, with a murder rate of 140 per 100,000. Astonishingly, more Salvadorans are now killed every day than during their country's 12-year civil war. Even in Costa Rica, long the region's most tranquil country, violence is reportedly on the rise" (1997).

13. Significantly enough, according to our interviews with the editor in chief and journalists of *La Revista Dominical* (a Sunday special of one of El Salvador's major newspapers, *La Prensa Gráfica*), which targets mostly readers between ages fifteen and twenty-five, a series of articles on young Salvadorans living in the United States, nicely illustrated with pictures, personal interviews, and individual histories, proved to be such a great success that it went on for several weekends.

14. In 1991, Guillermo Linares became the first Dominican to be elected to the New York City Council. Another Dominican, Adriano Espaillat, became the first Dominican to serve in the state assembly, after upsetting a sixteen-year incumbent in an upper Manhattan race in November 1997.

15. Dominicans own 20,000 New York businesses, including 70 percent of all small Latino grocery stores—New York's bodegas, which generate sales of $1.8 billion per year—and 90 percent of nonmedallion cabs, another multimillion dollar industry (Hernández, Rivera-Batiz, and Apodini 1996).

16. Also described well in the short article "Cash or Coffin (Dominicans in the U.S.)" in the *Economist*, 25 September 1993.

17. Irineo Tristán Montoya was accused of killing a border patrol officer along the U.S.–Mexico border in 1993. He was executed in Huntsville, Texas, on June 18, 1997.

18. An assertion that seems well supported by the facts. In surveying several official statements and media stories on the subject that were published in Mexico during June, we found that there was a strong humanitarian emphasis against the death penalty, the general ethnic discrimination suffered by Mexicans in the United States, the lack of access to a good defense on the part of Montoya, and the history of unequal relations between the United States and Mexico, with little or no reference whatsoever to the actual crimes that the accused had allegedly committed (Official Declaration by then Mexican Secretary of State [*Secretario de Relaciones Exteriores*] José Angel Gurria. *La Jornada*, Mexico City, June 11, 1997; Official Declaration by the Mexican State Department [*Secretaria de Relaciones Exteriores*]. *La Jornada*. Mexico City, June 19, 1997; *La Jornada*, June 11, p. 3, June 17, p. 3, and June 19, 1997; *Excelsior*, June 18, 1997).

19. See *Enfoque-Vision de Hoy: La guerra con Estados Unidos*. September 4, 1997. *Reforma* (Mexico).

20. A reality well illustrated by the lack of precise knowledge revealed in an official report on Colombia–U.S. relations in which the number of Colombian emigrants in the United States was estimated at around 1 million (IEPRI 1997). In 1990 the U.S. Census Bureau estimated that number at around 400,000 (including native and foreign-born), and as of 1997, the year in which the report was published, the number probably stood at 600,000.

21. For more than fifteen years, the Colombian drug lords have been smuggling cocaine by hiring human "mules" (called "internal body carriers" by DEA officials) to swallow as many as fifty condoms filled with the white powder, a method that despite its danger to the carrier remains the most common one (Speart 1995).

22. For example, when we surveyed one of Guatemala's major newspapers, *La Prensa Libre*, for ten days (August 20-30, 1997), we found two long articles and one short note on news and issues involving repatriation from Mexico, five long articles and three short notes on money laundering and drug-trafficking incidents, and not a single article or note on issues or events involving emigration to the United States.

23. An estimated 650,000 Guatemalan emigrants were living in southern Mexico in early 1996, whereas about 300,000 were living in the United States in the same period.

24. A flow that is likely to increase in the near future given the simple fact that Guatemala, with almost 11 million residents, is the most populous nation in Central America.

25. For good discussions of this topic in other Third World nations, see Fardmanesh 1991 and Kamas 1986.

26. See "El Salvador: Threat of Recession Calls Government's Economic Master Plan into Question." *Latin America Data Base-UTCAT. (LANIC-LADBUTA 5).* July 31, 1996.

27. The most well-known and popular Caribbean tropical music today, of presumably Cuban origin.

28. Actually, its renewed popularity has gone beyond Dominican audiences, and in 1995, for the first time in more than twenty years, a merengue song, *El Venado* (The Deer), became the biggest tropical single hit. In September 1995, the song reached No. 15 on *Billboard's* Hot Latin Tracks while climbing to No. 2 on the Tropical/Salsa chart, beating most Puerto Rican salsa songs of recent release (see Ross 1995).

29. Some link the "return" of merengue's popularity with the opposition to—and eventual demise of—the Balaguer regime that ruled the Dominican Republic for more than twenty-eight years. This may also be an indication of the rising cultural and political influence exerted in the Dominican Republic by expatriates in the United States. Large groups of refugees escaping the Balaguer regime contributed to the growth in numbers and influence of the Dominican community in New York for almost three decades (Ross 1994; Puleo 1997).

30. Contrary to this view, state governments as well as the national government have attempted to formalize their ties to Mexican emigrants living in the United States.

31. Government officials are still developing the regulations for implementing these changes. An official of the *Instituto Federal Electoral* (Federal Electoral Institute), the

agency that regulates voting and elections, informed us that the absentee ballot was unlikely to be available before the year 2000.

32. According to Matthews (1997), the "end of the Cold War has brought no mere adjustment among states but a novel redistribution of power among states, markets, and civil society. National governments are not simply losing autonomy in a globalizing economy. They are sharing powers (including political, social, and security roles at the core of sovereignty) with businesses, with international organizations, and with a multitude of citizens groups, known as nongovernmental organizations."

33. Note that chambers of commerce occupy a special place among both Latino and Latin American NGOs for, according to our findings, they are clearly at the forefront of establishing international and binational (between the United States and each Latin American country) connections.

34. Ernesto Zedillo Ponce de León, *"Admiramos lo que las comunidades hispanas han logrado para hacer valer sus principios." Con La Raza en Chicago. El Nacional.* August 4, 1997.

35. These evaluations are based on our interviews with Latin America consular representatives and Latino NGO leaders in Chicago, Houston, Los Angeles, Miami, New York, and Washington, D.C.

36. A report published by New York City authorities paints a very detailed demographic picture of the recent (early 1990s) citywide changes in immigration flows and ethnic and national urban settlement and occupational patterns. See *The Newest New Yorkers 1990–1994. An Analysis of Immigration to NYC in the Early 1990s.* December 1996. New York City Department of City Planning.

References

Aguayo, Sergio. 1991. *From the Shadows to Center Stage: Nongovernmental Organizations and Central American Refugee Assistance.* Hemispheric Migration Project, Center for Immigration Policy and Refugee Assistance. Washington, D.C.: Georgetown University.

Amiana N., Cristina. 1993. *Dominican Week in the United States.* New York and Washington, D.C.: La Semana Dominicana.

Bach, Robert L., and Doris Meissner. 1990. *America's Labor Market in the 1990s: What Role Should Immigration Play?* Washington, D.C.: Immigration Policy Project of the Carnegie Endowment for International Peace.

Bebbington, Anthony, and Graham Thiele. 1993. *Nongovernmental Organizations and the State in Latin America.* London: Routledge.

Carroll, Thomas S. 1987. *Supporting Grassroots Organizations.* Chicago: Lincoln Institute of Land Policy.

Castañeda, Jorge. 1994. *Three Challenges to U.S. Democracy: Accountability, Representativeness, and Intellectual Diversity.* Notre Dame, Ind.: University of Notre Dame Press.

Clough, Michael. 1994. "Grass-roots Policymaking: Say Good-bye to the 'Wise men' (US foreign policy leaders)." *Foreign Affairs* 73, no. 1: 2–6.

CUPULA (Colombianos Unidos Por Una Labor Activa). 1995. "Actualidad Colombiana." Chicago: Adelante-CUPULA.

de la Garza, Rodolfo O. 1980. "Chicanos and U.S. Foreign Policy: The Future of Chicano-Mexican Relations." *Western Political Quarterly* 33, no. 4: 571–82.

——— 1997a. "Foreign Policy Comes Home: The Domestic Consequences of the Program for Mexican Communities Living in Foreign Countries." In Rodolfo O. de la Garza and Jesús Velasco, eds., *Bridging the Border: Transforming Mexico–U.S. Relations*. Lanham, Md.: Rowman & Littlefield.

de la Garza, Rodolfo, Jerome Hernández, Angelo Falcón, F. Chris García, and John A. García. 1997b. "Mexican, Puerto Rican, and Cuban Foreign Policy Perspectives: A Test of Competing Explanations." In F. Chris Gracía, ed., *Pursuing Power: Latinos and the Political System*. Notre Dame, Ind.: University of Notre Dame Press.

DeSipio, Louis. 1996. "Special Friends: Consulate Efforts to Promote National Politics among Latin American Immigrants." Paper prepared for delivery at the annual meetings of the American Political Science Association, San Francisco, August 29–September 1.

DeSipio, Louis, Harry P. Pachon, et al. 1997. *America's Newest Voices: Colombians, Dominicans, Guatemalans and Salvadorans in the United States Examine Their Public Policy Needs*. Los Angeles, Calif.: NALEO Educational Fund and the Tomás Rivera Policy Institute.

——— 1997. *Constructing the Los Angeles Area Latino Mosaic: A Demographic Portrait of Guatemalans and Salvadorans in Los Angeles*. Claremont, Calif.: The Tomás Rivera Policy Institute and the NALEO Educational Fund.

——— 1997. *Constructing the New York Area Hispanic Mosaic: A Demographic Portrait of Colombians and Dominicans in New York*. Los Angeles, Calif.: NALEO Educational Fund and the Tomás Rivera Policy Institute.

——— 1997. *Diversifying the Los Angeles Area Latino Mosaic: Guatemalan and Salvadoran Leaders' Assessments of Community Public Policy Needs*. Claremont, Calif.: The Tomás Rivera Policy Institute and NALEO Educational Fund.

——— 1997. *Diversifying the New York Area Hispanic Mosaic: Colombian and Dominican Leaders' Assessments of Community Public Policy Needs* Los Angeles, Calif.: NALEO Educational Fund and the Tomás Rivera Policy Institute.

Edwards, Michael, and David Hulme. 1992. *Making a Difference: NGOs and Development in a Changing World*. London: Earthscan Publications.

Eisenstadt, Todd A. 1997. "The Rise of the Mexico Lobby in Washington: Even Further from God, and Even Closer to the United States." In Rodolfo O. de la Garza and Jesús Velasco, eds., *Bridging the Border: Transforming Mexico–U.S. Relations*. Lanham, Md.: Rowman & Littlefield.

Esman, Milton J. 1986. "Diasporas and International Relations." In Gabriel Sheffer, ed., *Modern Diasporas in International Politics*, 333–49. London: Croom-Helm.

Fardmanesh, Moshen. 1991. "Dutch Disease Economics and the Oil Syndrome: An Empirical Study." *World Development* 19, no. 6: 711–18.

Farkas, Steve, and Rodolfo de la Garza, et al. 1998. *Here to Stay: The Domestic and International Priorities of Latino Leaders*. Claremont, Calif.: Public Agenda and the Tomás Rivera Policy Institute.

Fishlow, Albert, and Stephan Haggard. 1992. *The United States and the Regionalisation of the World Economy.* Paris: OECD.

Gallegos, Herman E., and Michael O'Neill, eds. 1991. *Hispanics and the Nonprofit Sector.* New York: Foundation Center.

Gonzalez, Antonio, 1998. Seminar on "Advancing the Interests of African Americans, Asian Americans and Latinos." Sponsored by the Pacific Council on International Policy.

González Gutiérrez, Carlos. 1993. "The Mexican Diaspora in California: Limits and Possibilities for the Mexican Government." In Abraham F. Lowenthal and Katrina Burgess, eds., *Mexican-U.S. Relations: Conflict and Convergence.* Stanford, Calif.: Stanford University Press.

————— 1995. "La Organización de los Migrantes Mexicanos en Los Angeles: La Lealtad de los Oriundos." *Política Exterior* 46 (spring).

————— 1997. "Decentralized Diplomacy: The Role of Consular Offices in Mexico's Relation with Its Diaspora." In Rodolfo O. de la Garza and Jesús Velasco, eds., *Bridging the Border: Transforming Mexico–U.S. Relations.* Lanham, Md.: Rowman & Littlefield: 5–15.

Gress, Hans. 1996. "Interstate Cooperation and Territorial Representation in Intermestic Policies." *Publius* 26, no. 1: 53–72.

Guarnizo, Luis E. 1994. "Los Dominicanyorks: The Making of a Binational Society." *Annals of the American Academy of Political and Social Science* 533, (May): 70–87.

Hartlyn, Jonathan, Lars Schoultz, and Augusto Varas, eds. 1992. *The United States and Latin America in the 1990s: Beyond the Cold War.* Chapel Hill: University of North Carolina Press.

Hernández, Ramona, Francisco Rivera-Batiz, and Roberto Apodini. 1996. *Dominican New Yorkers: A Socioeconomic Profile.* Dominican Research Monographs. New York: CUNY Dominican Studies Institute.

Huntington, Samuel. 1996. "The West: Unique, Not Universal." *Foreign Affairs* 75, no. 6: 17–28.

————— 1997. "The Erosion of American National Interests." *Foreign Affairs* (September–October) 28–49.

IEPRI (Instituto de Estudios Políticos y Relaciones Internacionales) 1997. "Colombia: Una Nueva Sociedad en un Mundo Nuevo." In Alvaro Camacho Guizado, ed., *Análisis Político* (July). Bogotá: Universidad Nacional de Colombia.

Jaguaribe, Helio. 1991. *The U.S. after the Cold War: A View from the South Cone.* Sao Paulo, Brazil: University of Sao Paulo.

Jones-Correa, Michael. 1995. "New Directions for Latinos as an Ethnic Lobby in U.S. Foreign Policy." *Harvard Journal of Hispanic Policy* 9, no. 4: 47–85.

Kamas, Linda. 1986. "Dutch Disease Economics and the Colombian Export Boom." *World Development* 14, no. 2: 1177–97.

López, José Roberto, and Mitchell A. Seligson. 1990. "Small Business Development in El Salvador: The Impact of Remittances." Washington, D.C.: Commission for the Study of International Migration and Cooperative Economic Development.

Lowenthal, Abraham F. 1992. "The Intermestic Hemisphere." *New Perspectives Quarterly* 9, no. 3: 37–41.

Matthews, Jessica T. 1997. "Power Shift." *Foreign Affairs* 76, no. 1: 35–52.

McFadden, Robert. 1997. "Limits on Cash Transactions Cut Drug-Money Laundering (Treasury Department order imposing $750-per-transaction limit on remittance shops suspected of wiring illicit money)." *New York Times*, March 11: A1.

Melville, Thomas, and Marjorie Melville. 1991. *Guatemala: The Politics of Land Ownership*. New York: The Free Press.

Molineau, Harold. 1990. *U.S. Policy toward Latin America: From Regionalism to Globalism*. 2nd ed. Boulder, Colo.: Westview Press.

Monteforte Toledo, Mario. 1997. *La Frontera Móvil*. México: Universidad Nacional Autónoma de México and Guatemala: Naciones Unidas-Ministerio de Cultura y Deportes.

Muñoz, Heraldo. 1996. *Latin American Nations in World Politics*. 2nd ed. Boulder, Colo.: Westview Press.

Nayyar, Deepak. 1994. "International Labor Movements, Trade Flows and Migration Transitions: A Theoretical Perspective." *Asian and Pacific Migration Journal* 3, no. 1: 31–47.

Pastor, Robert A. 1992. *Whirlpool: U.S. Foreign Policy towards Latin America and the Caribbean*. Princeton: Princeton University Press.

Puleo, Gus. 1997. "Merengue and the Politics of Nationhood and Identity in the Dominican Republic." *Latin American Issues: The Caribbean(s) Redefined* 13: 105–25.

Ross, Karl. 1994. "Merengue Star Mixes Music, Politics." *Billboard* 106, no. 36: 52.

——— 1995. "Merengue Hit Fuels Passion, Maybe Murder, in Caribbean." *Billboard* 107, no. 40: 14–16.

Salamon, Lester M. 1994. "The Rise of the Nonprofit Sector." *Foreign Affairs* 73, no. 4: 22–45.

Shain, Yossi. 1994. "Ethnic Diasporas and U.S. Foreign Policy." *Political Science Quarterly* 109, no. 5: 811–842.

——— 1995. "Multicultural Foreign Policy." *Foreign Policy* 2, no. 100: 69–86.

Sheffer, Gabriel. 1994. "Ethno-National Diasporas and Security." *Survival* 36, no. 1.

Shifter, Michael. 1997. *Central America: Current Trends and Recommendations for U.S. Policy*. Testimony prepared for Hearing of the Subcommittee on the Western Hemisphere, House Committee on International Relations, Washington, D.C., June 25. Inter-American Dialogue Policy Brief. Washington, D.C.: USDOS.

Siri, Gabriel, and Pedro Abelardo Delgado. 1995. *Uso Productivo de las Remesas Familiares en El Salvador*. San Salvador, El Salvador: FUSADES.

Smith, Robert. 1996. "Mixteca in New York; New York in Mixteca." *Report on the Americas* 26, no. 1: 39–43.

Speart, Jessica. 1995. "The New Drug Mules." *The New York Times Magazine,* June 11:44.

The World Bank. 1995. CD-Rom Database: Socio-Economic Text Access and Retrieval System. New York: International Bank for Reconstruction and Development/The World Bank.

Tokatlian, Juán G., and Bruce M. Bagley. 1990. *Economía y Política del Narcotráfico*. 1st ed. Bogotá, Colombia: CEREC.

Ullman, Richard H. 1995. "A Late Recovery (President Clinton's Foreign Policy)." *Foreign Policy* 2, no. 101: 76–80.

U.S. Bureau of the Census. 1980. *1980 Census of Population*. Washington, D.C.: U.S. Government Printing Office.

U.S. Bureau of the Census. 1990. *1990 Census of Population.* Washington, D.C.: U.S. Government Printing Office.

U.S. Bureau of the Census. 1997. *U.S. International Trade Statistics.* Washington, D.C.: U.S. Government Printing Office.

U.S. Bureau of the Census. 1994. " The Foreign-Born Population: 1994." In *Current Population Survey,* 20–486. Washington, D.C.: U.S. Government Printing Office.

U.S. Department of Commerce. 1996. *Population Projections of the United States by Age, Sex, Race and Hispanic Origin: 1995–2050.* Washington, D.C.: Department of Commerce, U.S. Government Printing Office.

Van Klaveren, Alberto. 1992. *America Latina en el Mundo.* Santiago, Chile: Prospel.

Velasco, Jesús. 1997. "Selling Ideas, Buying Influence: México and American Think Tanks in the Promotion of NAFTA." In Rodolfo O. de la Garza and Jesús Velasco, eds., *Bridging the Border: Transforming Mexico–U.S. Relations.* Lanham, Md.: Rowman & Littlefield.

PART III

HOME COUNTRY RESPONSES TO "FAMILY TIES AND ETHNIC LOBBIES"

4

The Exceptionality of Colombians

Fernando Cepeda Ulloa

One of the most telling findings of the study "Family Ties and Ethnic Lobbies: Latino Relations with Latin America" is that it shows how Latinos differ from one another. One might think that Latinos living in a society such as the United States would tend to resemble each other, almost to the point of appearing to be identical. But this and other studies indicate something very different: Colombian immigrants to the United States behave differently than do Salvadorans, Mexicans, or Dominicans; their respective governments relate differently to their expatriate populations; and, of course, these differences reflect the political or economic circumstances that gave rise to the emigration.

Colombia has not generated massive migratory streams toward the United States that are the result of an intolerable dictatorship, a violent revolution, or a profound economic crisis. And although Colombia has suffered from persistent violence, worsened at times by narco-terrorism, neither this situation nor any other circumstance has precipitated a stampede to the United States. Rather, the emigration has been a constant process induced by a longing to live better and by the undeniable attractiveness of the U.S. lifestyle to the middle and lower classes.

Colombians do not stand out in their ability to create organizations to maximize the benefits they can obtain from the different levels of government in the United States. This is understandable because Colombians have more trust in client and family relations than in institutional ones. What is most important to a Colombian is what friends or relatives can do for him or her. Colombians greatly distrust institutions.

These behavioral patterns do not disappear when Colombians come to the United States, or even after they live here a while. In the absence of advantages resulting from privilege, there is nothing on which to rely in Colombia or the United States except help from friends or relatives. This reliance becomes, however, much more important for expatriates.

Domestic Politics

This somewhat tribal behavior is reflected in the attitude of the Colombian emigrants toward the government of the receiving country and toward their own government. It is difficult for Colombians, at certain levels, to convince themselves that they have rights and that they are able to exercise them. The concept of *favors* still dominates that of *rights*. Thus, it is hard for Colombians to believe that equal treatment exists. Their tendency is to look for a connection, in other words, a friend or relative—almost an accomplice.

This being the case, it would be very surprising to learn that there are Colombians who would organize in the United States to obtain, through institutional means, benefits or opportunities that should be open to legal residents. It would be more surprising still to find out that they would organize in order to influence or orient U.S. politics or international politics or anything having to do with Colombia's politics. In short, it is difficult to see how behavior corresponding to a culture of subjugation could, in a new geographical context, transform itself into a culture of participation.

It would be worthwhile to investigate the circumstances under which such a transformation could be produced. Theories about the circumstances that give rise to the creation of a pressure group also are valid in the case of migrants. Imitation has an impact, and it is clear that exceptional circumstances create exceptional leaders. Natural disasters, for example, can trigger feelings of solidarity, revitalize faltering organizations, and create new associations. Unfortunately, these reactions are probably not sustainable. If this is what happens domestically, then it is not hard to believe that Colombian immigrants' initiative or ability to respond is the same or worse.

Foreign Politics

The formulation of a Colombian foreign policy has been reserved to a very few, and the debate has been heated. One example serves to illustrate this situation. Without a doubt, the major crisis in Colombian–U.S. relations occurred during the Samper administration (1994–1998). In the next presidential campaign, although two women who had served as ministers of foreign relations under Samper were running (Noemí Sanín for the presidency, María Emma Mejía for the vice presidency), bilateral relations were not debated—and this in spite of four decertifications[1] and other sanctions that gravely affected the country's international standing. How could one reasonably hope for different behavior on the part of Colombians living in the United States?

The study that we are discussing notes, in fact, that, according to a Colombian diplomat, the U.S. embassy in Colombia even suggested that the Colombian government urge Colombian immigrants to organize against the decertification. How could one hope, then, for different behavior on the part of the Colombians who live in the United States? One of the few examples of Latinos who support the interests of their native governments instead of those of the United States is the professional and elite groups that tried to influence the U.S. government to support Colombia's certification—doubtless as a way of improving their status and image in the United States.

In Colombia, the crisis in bilateral relations (1941–1998) generated an ephemeral interest in the economic sector and a somewhat lesser interest in the academic sector. Apathy is now equal to or worse than it once was, despite the fact that the peace process remains inextricably tied to the illicit drug trade and, as a consequence, to the national security interests of the United States, not to mention military aid and its complicated relationship with the subject of human rights. Only a very few Colombians worry about these troublesome areas; thus it is natural that the situation of Colombian immigrants in the United States is not debated either, nor does it have a place in policy formulation.

The study refers to initiatives that affect Colombian immigrants: (1) the consular obligation to maintain contact with Colombian prisoners in U.S. jails (including discussions of their repatriation); (2) the right of dual citizenship granted by the 1991 Constitution; (3) the right of those living abroad to vote in Senate elections beginning in 1998 (Art. 171, Constitución Política, 1991); (4) the right to vote in presidential elections; and (5) the possibility of creating a special constituency so that expatriates are represented in the Chamber of Deputies (Art. 176). On occasion, unsuccessful attempts have been made to implement programs like those Spain has developed for its immigrants. There has been talk of opening SENA offices for vocational training in countries where there are significant colonies of Colombians, for example, the United States, Venezuela, and Ecuador.[2] Also, lawyers have been hired to intercede on behalf of Colombian prisoners in foreign jails. Government officials have also discussed promoting the organization of Colombian immigrants.

As I have noted, however, Colombians are not known for their willingness to join voluntary organizations, or to participate in them, or to contribute to their maintenance. Thus, allowing immigrants to participate in the electoral process in Colombia and the creation of a special constituency to assure the representation of Colombian residents abroad (Art. 176) might go a long way toward changing Colombians' natural reluctance to organize. The Colombian government might be interested in promoting this, as is recommended in the report of the Colombian–U.S. Commission. Additionally, the Commission report notes that

> it is understood that the principal mission of the consulates is to take care of Colombian nationals and to promote commerce. But given the difficulties that the ambassador has in moving from one place to another, the mission should be to provide a source of information and support. For this to happen, the consuls and support personnel must be foreign service professionals and have periodic, at least twice yearly, general meetings with the ambassador and with the directors of the Ministry. (Tokatlian 1998, 62)

The Commission is not optimistic about the success of Colombian immigrants in improving their personal situation or in assisting Colombia. The Commission sees more possibilities in what the Colombian colony can do in states like Florida or in cities such as Miami: "It is necessary to ally ourselves with sectors of American society that have interests to protect through ties to the country [Colombia]" (Tokatlian 1998, 55). Anthony P. Maingot conducted a study for the Commission and pointed out the key issues affecting Colombians residing in the United States. He advised the government to concentrate more on Florida than on Washington in view of the fact that the former has the third-largest Colombian-origin population and is second in growth rate. He pointed out the campaign to persuade Congress to certify Colombia that originated from Miami's World Trade Center. The attempt failed, but, says Maingot, "it did contribute in that decertification did not include any economic sanctions" (in Tokatlian 1998, 321).

Although the definitive foreign policy decisions are made and will continue to be made in Washington, the case of Colombia—which must take into account the population's generalized perceptions—requires a different strategy. What Colombian society needs is for Colombians in the Unite States with legitimate interests in Colombia to try to assume leadership positions in the governmental bodies of the cities and states where they reside. Because no other state has a greater interest in good relations with Colombia than Florida, the effort should begin there. The economies of Colombia and Florida complement each other; there is harmony, not competition, between their economic interests; and there is a wish to change Colombian immigrants' image and perceptions (Maingot 1998, 320).

Christopher Mitchell of New York University is not optimistic about the chances of this behavioral shift occurring. After analyzing various successes and failures of diverse Latino groups in the United States, he concludes:

> There is very limited research into the sociology, the objectives, and the organization of Colombians in the United States. But including the little scientific information available, our analysis suggests that it will be difficult for Colombian migrants in the United States to influence the policy of Washington toward their country of origin.
>
> Let's examine their record and potential for lobbying in light of the six variables we have just reviewed.
>
> Generally, Colombian immigrants have not articulated a vigorous and effective message to send legislators concerned with U.S. foreign policy. On the relatively rare occasions on which Colombians have mobilized with this objective, they have looked for fair treatment and a better understanding of Colombia and the many challenges that confront our country. Messages such as these give rise to supportive responses from a government that is a source of migrants. It has been difficult for the migrants of many nations to formulate and ask questions about what constitutes fair treatment and how the U.S. government, to a great extent, tends to seek allies from among other interest groups. Colombian immigrants could search for supporters among the investors (actual as well as potential) who do business with Colombia, academicians and students, Peace Corps volunteers who have returned after working in Colombia, and groups of immigrants from other Western Hemisphere nations. There might be an opportunity to join Mexican American groups that only recently have experienced the bad image that some U.S. media project about immigrants from nations that are involved in international drug trafficking.
>
> The Colombians in the United States should, however, probably wait for political changes in their own country before they draw up a convincing message that is compatible with the present ideology of the United States and one that will allow them to diminish the political stigma that often affects them. It would be totally unrealistic to hope that the drug traffic will be eradicated in Colombia, as it is happening inside the United States. In spite of everything, an effective lobbying effort on the part of Colombian immigrants in the United States requires an administration in Colombia that is convincingly separated from the narcotics trade and whose authority can be distinguished from the power of the drug dealers (in Tokatlian 1998, 162–163).

It would be convenient to compare what is happening with other Latino groups, particularly in Latin America. It would not, in fact, be surprising if the case of Colombian migrants in Venezuela or Ecuador were found to be similar. The illegal immigration status of many Colombians naturally makes them unwilling to be visible. The fear of deportation or other types of sanctions is very great.

An example of the Colombian government's new interest in emigrants is the Program for the Promotion of Colombian Communities Abroad (PPCCE). The PPCCE includes a program that keeps track of Colombians who reside abroad; preservation of national culture; legal advice for those detained in foreign prisons; professionalization of the consular body; and a census and timely studies to determine the size and the needs of the dispersed immigrant population.

Luis Eduardo Guarnizo and Arturo Ignacio Sánchez paint, at least in New York, a more optimistic picture:

> Mayor Rudolph Giuliani's pro-immigrant stand formed part of the campaign to achieve his reelection. For example, in a recent celebration of National Independence Day in July in Flushing Meadows' Corona Park in Queens, the mayor of the city, Rudolph W. Giuliani, various candidates for the city council, and a congresswoman addressed approximately 200,000 Colombians and eulogized Colombian nationality and presented symbolic proclamations of recognition. Besides their instrumental character, the presence of these politicians in this event underlines the fact that Colombians are recognized and appreciated for more than their image of the drug trafficker and the undesirable. Equally as important is the fact that it has been more than 15 years since the last studies of Colombians in New York were done, new studies have begun in the last two years in the United States. (Tokatlian 1998, 323)

Individualism, their reticence to participate, the tradition of friendship, the ability to survive in the most adverse circumstances—in Colombia or abroad—geographic regionalism, family sentiment, all contribute to differentiate the Colombian from other Latinos. Unfortunately, the stigma of drugs makes relationships with Americans or other Latinos more difficult—even though such relationships may be for civic purposes—and strengthens distrust among compatriots because of the implicit risk of associating with people who may be involved in the criminal drug trade.

We must wait for better times. Low-cost and easy means of communication for Colombians in Miami and New York, the peace process in Colombia, the growing presence of guerrilla conflict, and situations such as that in New York with the election of Giuliani or the opportunity to participate in the Colombian electoral process can, together with greater action by the Colombian government, transform the role of the Colombian community in the United States and make it more participatory in domestic and international matters. For now, though, it is naive to expect from Colombians in the United States a political culture different from the one that has inspired their behavior in Colombia.

Notes

This chapter was translated from Spanish by Carolyn P. Dunlap, TRPI Research Associate and Associate Instructor, Department of Spanish and Portuguese, University of Texas at Austin.

1. *Decertification* refers to the decision by the U.S. Congress to deny aid because of its assessment that Colombia had failed to effectively combat narco-trafficking.

2. SENA is the Colombian government's vocational training agency.

References

Camacho, Álvaro, ed., 1997. *Colombia: Una Nueva Sociedad en un Mundo Nuevo*. Bógota Instituto de Estudios Politicos y Relaciones Internacionales, Universidad Nacional de Colombia.

Maingot, Anthony P. 1998. "Colombia y el estado federado de la florida." In Tokatlian, Juan Gabriel, comp. *Colombia y Estados Unidos: problemas y perspectivas*. Bogota: Tercer Mundo.

Mitchell, Christopher. 1998. "Una Comparison de los Esfuerzos de los grupos de migrantes del hemispherio occidental para influenciar la politica estadounidense hacia sus países de origen. In Tokatlian, Juan Gabriel, comp. *Colombia y Estados Unidos: problemas y perspectivas*. Bogota: Tercer Mundo.

Tokatlian, Juan Gabriel, comp. 1998. *Colombia y Estados Unidos: problemas y perspectivas*. Bogota: Tercer Mundo.

5

The Political Role of Dominicans Residing in the United States

Bernardo Vega

T he Cold War that began in 1947 has ended, but we are confronted with another Cold War: the fight against drugs, money laundering, and illegal immigration.[1]

The United States used to consider the Caribbean as a geopolitically important strategic zone because of the Panama Canal and the danger of Soviet-Cuban penetration. The zone is still considered strategically important, but now because drugs from South America are in transit across it and because of the large number of illegal immigrants near the coasts. Because of these factors, the components of the U.S.–Dominican agenda are essentially related to policing, the fight against narco-trafficking, and illegal immigration; the extradition to the United States of Dominicans against whom U.S. courts have issued warrants; the deportation of delinquent Dominicans back to the Dominican Republic; the negotiation of agreements permitting American boats and planes to enter the territorial waters and skies of Caribbean and Central American countries to search for drugs and illegal immigrants; and pacts against money laundering.

It is important to emphasize that these issues greatly influence the U.S. agenda. Geographical proximity makes these issues especially cogent. The refugees who look for a way to leave Albania illegally, for example, are not as important to U.S. foreign policy as are the illegal Caribbean emigrants, for the simple reason that the latter can, and do, come with relative ease to the United States. Thus, with every passing day it is more difficult to differentiate U.S. foreign and domestic policy from one another.

From the Dominican point of view, the biggest worry in bilateral relations is the damage that the immigration laws of 1996 may inflict on, first, the Dominican community in the United States, and, second, the national economy. The diminishing possibilities for legal migration to the United States, the danger of deportations of Dominicans who are legal residents, the reduction in welfare resources, and even efforts to eliminate rent control in New York are all matters of extraordinary importance not only for the Dominican diaspora but also for those Dominicans who remain at home. Furthermore, there is widespread ignorance about this issue.

According to the U.S. Immigration and Naturalization Service, some 75,000 Dominicans live in the United States without any kind of documentation; they barely represent 1.5 percent of all of the undocumented immigrants in the United States, however. Although undocumented Dominicans contribute very little to the major issues facing the United States, a massive deportation of these Dominicans would be traumatic for the Dominican Republic in human and economic terms. While Cubans, Haitians, and Central Americans now benefit from laws that impede mass deportation, Dominicans do not receive any special treatment whatsoever.

The Role of the Dominican American

The new U.S. agenda regarding the Dominican Republic concentrates on issues that form part of the domestic politics of the United States and that also have been drawn from important components of U.S. foreign policy. Thus Dominican Republic–related policy concentrates on immigration and narco-trafficking, rather than on topics exclusively about external politics, for example, hemispheric defense, the fight against the Communists in the 1950s, and the increase in NATO membership. Purely domestic considerations, therefore, more and more are affecting the formulation of foreign policy. The very strong immigration laws passed in an election year—1996—are a good example. Out of the immigration laws passed in that year grew the necessity for positive domestic pressures to influence the design of the North American bilateral agenda. The Cuban American and Haitian communities have since achieved some influence over the design of American policies toward Havana and Port-au-Prince, but the Dominican American community has yet to play a similar role.

It is important to note that, after Mexicans and Cubans, Dominicans are the largest Western Hemisphere group to gain U.S. citizenship since 1996. Between 1992 and 1995, some 10,500 Dominicans per year became American citizens and thus earned the right to vote. President Fernandez was wise when, in 1996, he urged Dominicans residing legally in the United States to become U.S. citizens. A constitutional amendment similar to one passed in Mexico some two years earlier assured Dominicans that they would not lose their Dominican citizenship after they became U.S. citizens. The potential for great numbers of Dominican-born U.S. citizens is high, because between 1992 and 1996, an average of 43,500 Dominicans became U.S. citizens, that is, four times more than those who nationalized themselves.[2] In 1996, Dominicans occupied sixth place among all legal immigrants to the United States; only Mexico sent more immigrants from this hemisphere. In 1998, the first year in which an affidavit of support for reunification of families was required, visas conceded to Dominicans were reduced by some 40 percent.

By contributing to candidates, forming pressure groups, writing their members of Congress, and running for office, Dominican Americans can influence the design of U.S. policy toward the Dominican Republic. At present, one state congressman and one city manager, both in New York, are of Dominican origin. The Dominican Embassy in Washington has formed dozens of diverse groups of Dominican Americans to send letters to Congress asking for support for the textile equality project. This type of grassroots action is far more effective than ambassadorial speech making. All serious candidates for mayor of New York visit Santo Domingo; New York's congressional delegation, as exemplified by Charles Rangel also recognizes the importance of the Dominican vote.

In terms of wielding political influence, it is unfortunate that Dominican Americans, who are overwhelmingly Democratic, are concentrated in states in which the Democratic Party is strong. Consequently, their vote does not have the clout it would have if they were living in a state in which a specific interest group's vote could swing an election either way. If South Dakota, for example, had a Dominican community the size of New York's, surely its senator would be of Dominican origin.

The Growing Importance of the Hispanic Vote

During the past ten years, the number of Hispanics in the United States has grown some 53 percent, a rate seven times higher than that of the rest of the U.S. population. Today, Hispanics constitute ten percent of the total U.S. population: 64 percent are Mexican, 10 percent are Puerto Rican, 4 percent are Cuban, and the remaining 22 percent are people of other origins, including Dominicans. Almost half (48%) of the Hispanics are under age twenty-five, which indicates that the growth rate of the Hispanic population will continue to be very high. According to census projections, by 2005 the Hispanic population will be about 32 million, making it the second largest minority group after African Americans. By 2035, that is, in the equivalent of a generation, one out of every five North Americans will be of Hispanic origin. Because of this expected growth, Hispanics are chanting, "We shall overwhelm."

The Hispanic Vote's Effect on U.S. Elections

In the 1996 elections, there were 8 million Hispanics eligible to vote; of these, 6.6 million were registered, some 30 percent more than those registered to vote in the 1992 elections. Around 4 million Hispanics, or 60 percent of those registered, did in fact vote, a much higher rate than the national average of 47 percent.[3] This appears to indicate that Hispanics have a higher level of political consciousness than the rest of the population. About 72 percent of the Hispanic vote was cast for Democrats; only around 21 percent voted for Republicans. The overall Hispanic vote was crucial in states such as Florida and California, as Hispanics represented potential swing voters. There exists an erroneous belief that the Cuban vote is decisive in Florida, when really it is the Hispanic vote, that is, Cubans and non–Cuban Latinos, that counts.

More Hispanics registered and voted in the elections of 1996 in reaction to the laws passed in that year that negatively affected immigration and welfare issues. There are now indications that the Republican leadership regrets its stand concerning these two matters. It is no coincidence that in 1997, Congress, with Republican support, restored the welfare benefits of legal immigrants over age sixty, thanks to a publicity campaign in which the desperate cases of various elderly Dominicans residing in New York were cited. The Hispanic vote increased 29 percent between 1992 and 1996 and, among other things, resulted in a substantial increase in the number of congressmembers of Hispanic origin. The Hispanic Caucus increased to seventeen in 1996, and there were three Hispanics in President Clinton's first-term (1992–1996) cabinet.

The Hispanic Presence in U.S. Agriculture

Some 42 percent of agricultural laborers in the United States are Hispanic. They are concentrated in fruit and vegetable harvesting and follow the harvest. The so-called Latinization of rural America is concentrated in areas where harvest requires intense hand labor, as opposed to crops that are harvested by machine, such as corn, soy, and wheat. Some 670,000 Hispanics work in agriculture. These numbers suggest the importance of the Dominican Republic's participation in American temporary guest workers programs. One has only to look at the Jamaicans who cut cane in Florida and who might in the future harvest coffee in Puerto Rico and the harvest of fruits and vegetables by Dominicans on the East Coast of the United States. The use of Jamaican and Dominican temporary workers in these areas may diminish if Taiwan, as its chancellor recently declared, imports temporary Central American workers to substitute for workers from the Philippines and Thailand because of the relationship those countries have with China.

The Latino Attitude toward Welfare

There is an erroneous perception—almost as widespread and pernicious as the "Black Legend,"[4] which the English used to justify their struggles against Spain and their colonies in the Americas—that all Latinos favor continued dependence on welfare. Studies, however, prove that non–Puerto Rican Hispanics living in Queens depend 50 percent *less* on welfare than do Puerto Ricans living in the Bronx. According to a survey published by the Hispanic Federation of New York in summer 1999, 69 percent of Dominicans and 58 percent of other Hispanics (except Puerto Ricans) support a five-year limit on welfare payments. This implies that Dominicans do not maintain a parasitic link with the mechanisms of state assistance. It also indicates Hispanics are not of one voice regarding major policy issues, and that many hold views similar to those of the American mainstream.

The Political Organization
of Dominican Americans

It is important that Dominican Americans play an increasingly active role in U.S. politics, to defend not only their own interests, but also those of their country of origin. The big question is how to better organize this community so that its political influence keeps growing. I do not pretend to have the answer, but I can begin by mentioning what I believe should *not* be done.

I do not believe in the Haitian formula of creating a Ministry of Diaspora, as such a ministry in the Dominican Republic would imply that Dominican Americans see themselves as affected by Dominican political phenomena. Nor do I believe in the creation of an organization that depends on the Dominican embassy in Washington or the consulate in New York because, sooner or later, such an organization would become politicized and would be used for propagandistic ends. Nor do I believe it feasible to include the Dominican political parties in this organization, as it would run the same risk of politicization.

Perhaps the most effective and lasting means of politically organizing Dominican Americans would be through a process of self-management, created and developed inside their own community—perhaps even the unification of currently existing institutions inside this community. At the embassy in Washington I have begun to draw up a list of private, civil, nonprofit Dominican institutions in the United States whose objectives are typical. There are a surprising quantity and variety of such institutions. One such institution represents the entire community and could perhaps play a leading role. I refer to the Catholic Church. We should ask ourselves whether any institution that represents the interests of the Dominican American community must have an office in Washington. Could it not simply establish a liaison in Washington? And should it not be linked to currently existing institutions with common objectives.

National Council de la Raza

One of the institutions that could help politically animate the Dominican American community is the National Council of la Raza (NCLR), a private, nonprofit, nonpartisan organization created in 1968. It now includes some 20,000 Hispanic groups. Although it began as an organization whose objective was to protect Hispanics of Mexican origin, it is considering expanding its operations to the city of New York and to other Hispanic groups. Its two primary functions are (1) to analyze policies proposed by Washington and by the states in order to influence political decisions that affect its members; and (2) to mobilize voters, especially during elections, through campaigns linked to specific topics (e.g., immigration or welfare) that affect its members. An indicator of NCLR's political potency is that both Al Gore and Richard Gephardt, leading future Democratic presidential hopefuls, both spoke at the NCLR annual convention. The president of Mexico also attended.

The Mexican Experience

Dominican efforts to increase their political influence and influence U.S. policies affecting the Dominican Republic could learn from how Mexicans have dealt with similar issues. Until 1990 the Mexican government ascribed absolutely no importance to its community in the United States, nor to organizations like NCLR. NAFTA negotiations and the awareness of the importance of the Mexican American vote in the United States finally moved the Mexican government to create, in 1990, the Programa para las Comunidades Mexicanas en el Extranjero (Program for Mexican Communities Abroad). Although its stated objective is the incorporation of Mexican immigrants into the Mexican nation, which includes all Mexicans everywhere, it also has another unstated objective: to influence decisions made in Washington through Mexicans residing in the United States. The program considers multiculturalism to be the source of strength and not of weakness and includes the following:

- the promotion of exports through sales to the Mexican market in the United States;
- the promotion of conational visits to Mexico, like the visits of *Dominicanos ausentes* (Dominican emigrants);
- the education of adults in the United States;
- the education of children of immigrants;
- the facilitation of accrediting courses and diplomas so that Mexican children can continue their studies in Mexico and vice versa;
- the promotion of sport competitions;
- cultural programs, including traveling exhibitions; and
- the promotion of business through the Hispanic Chambers of Commerce.

One of NCLR's major accomplishments to date has been the preparation of a database of community leaders of Mexican origin in the United States. This database is used to send letters to members of Congress and other political leaders. In addition, a medal has been created that is awarded annually to someone who expends exceptional effort on behalf of the Mexican community in the United States. NCLR-sponsored publications include a newspaper entitled *La Paloma* and a bulletin entitled *Raices.* NCLR or some other Latino organization should be encouraged to produce publications like these, tailored to the Dominican community, for mass distribution in New York.

Finally, these objectives complement one another. The financing of Mexico's program should come as much from Mexican businesses with interests in the United States as from U.S. businesses with interests in Mexico, with contributions from the Mexican Secretary of Foreign Relations itself. Similarly, the Dominican government and private sector should together fund these types of programs for Dominicans in the United States.

The Experience of Other Ethnic Groups

The Cuban American community has acquired great importance in the political process. The Haitian community, through the Black Congressional Caucus, has succeeded in pressuring the U.S. government for the return of President Jean-Bertrand Aristide, even to the point of armed intervention. President Clinton's wish to include Lithuania in NATO may be related to a desire to secure the support of the Lithuanian community in Chicago before the primaries. The role of Jewish groups in the determination of U.S. foreign policy is well documented. The Irish community also greatly influences the U.S. attitude toward violence in their homeland. The Armenians have established an office in Washington to advance their interests.

If it is to have the same impact on U.S.–Dominican relations as the above groups have on U. S. policies toward their respective homelands, the Dominican community in the United States has a long way to go. Clearly, a major challenge is the creation of a nonpartisan agenda reflecting its own interests such as immigration and social service issues. Dominican Americans may also influence matters that affect the homeland such as more favorable textile and sugar agreements, foreign debt issues, and the promotion of private U.S. investment, among other things.

Dominicans should not underestimate their ability. Who would have thought thirty years ago that there would be more than forty Dominican baseball players in the Major Leagues? It could easily happen that soon there will be senators, federal officers, mayors, and governors of Dominican origin, and by 2044, the date of the Dominican Republic's bicentennial, a president of Dominican origin in the White House. Why not?

Notes

This chapter was translated from Spanish by Carolyn P. Dunlap, TRPI Research Associate and Associate Instructor, Department of Spanish and Portuguese, University of Texas at Austin.

1. Ambassador Vega's essay goes beyond responding to the major findings of this study as reported in chapter 3. Instead, his essay may be better understood as a description of the future role that Latinos will play in U.S.–Latin American relations. As such, it combines the recognition that domestic issues will be salient to immigrants with the expectation that Dominicans and other Latinos will remain closely involved with their home country's political agenda.

2. Editors' note: There may be a difference between Mexican law and Dominican law on this point. Mexicans who become U.S. citizens retain their nationality but lose their citizenship and may not vote in Mexican elections. Domincans who naturalize apparently may continue to vote in Dominican elections.

3. Editor's note: Hispanic turnout in 1996 was significantly lower and much less significant than is argued here. See Rodolfo O. de la Garza and Louis DeSipio, eds., *Awash in the Mainstream: Latinos and the 1996 Election*, Boulder, Colo.: Westview Press.

4. The "Black Legend" refers to the self-serving English depiction of the Spanish conquest of the "New World" as having been motivated by greed and religious fanaticism and left nothing of value in the conquered lands.

6

El Salvador's Relations with Salvadoran Emigrants

René León

T he Salvadorans currently residing in the United States, for the most part, left El Salvador during the 1980s, because of a twelve-year period of internal conflict. Salvadorans living in the United States are not only very united and hardworking, but also active participants in the U.S. economy. Additionally, they do not forget their roots and are involved in assuring the well-being of their respective communities back home.

The contribution of Salvadorans living in the United States to the home country can be measured economically, politically, and culturally, among other ways. In economic terms, their importance is great. In 1997, remittances sent to El Salvador from Salvadorans living abroad amounted to U.S. $1.3 billion, which amounts to 10 percent of El Salvador's GDP, or 65 percent of exports. These remittances not only contribute to the overall economy of the country, but they greatly affect the lifestyle of families who have seen their purchasing power increased by the remittances.

The majority of remittances are sent in small amounts to family members to cover basic needs. Furthermore, El Salvador's Legislative Assembly is currently studying the feasibility of money-laundering legislation, with the aid of the U.S. government.

In social and cultural terms, Salvadoran emigrants have had both a positive and a negative impact in their home country. On the one hand, it is believed that the steady and increasing deportation of Salvadoran gang members (*maras*) back to El Salvador since 1998 has contributed to violence in El Salvador. This phenomenon has the potential of greatly affecting the country's and region's future developments. The maras problem is only one aspect of this phenomenon.

The report we are discussing here reflects some of the positive contributions of Salvadoran emigrants to their home country, although I feel that it does not go into enough depth regarding their contributions to U.S. society. In Washington, D.C., for example, there are at least six community associations organized by Salvadoran hometowns. These regularly raise funds to help their communities at home. With these funds some organizations have sent an ambulance, built a stadium, and paved roads.

The report also deals with Salvadoran perceptions of Salvadorans living in the United States. The latter are admired for their economic success, for their contributions to Salvadoran society, and for their social progress in the United States. A major newspaper in El Salvador recently reported on a Salvadoran immigrant in California who won the Democratic primary for a seat in the state Senate.

It might still be too early to accurately measure the impact on the political life of El Salvador of Salvadorans living abroad. Though the Salvadoran electoral system does not permit absentee voting, neither does it prohibit the raising of funds abroad for the financing of political campaigns in El Salvador. Salvadorans living abroad may also affect the homeland's political life by influencing their relatives' votes. Furthermore, absentee ballot legislation may still be enacted.

Salvadorans living in the United States constitute 20 percent of the population of El Salvador. This report gives us some figures to work with, but, unfortunately, immigration figures vary greatly, depending on the source. For example, the 1972 census shows El Salvador's population at 5.5 million, whereas the 1992 census, despite a 2.1 percent annual population growth, gives the same figure.

What has the government of El Salvador done for its citizens living in the United States? The protection and well-being of Salvadorans living in the United States—roughly 20 percent of our population—is a priority for the embassy and for the government of El Salvador. The government has instituted a number of policies and programs that address their needs.

A recent and ambitious project that the Ministry of Foreign Affairs is undertaking is the modernization of the eleven U.S. consulates. This modernization implies, on the one hand, a streamlining of procedures that will lead to more efficient and prompt consular services, and, on the other, that work is being done to strengthen the consulate's ties to the community it serves.

The embassy has an open-door policy toward the Salvadoran community. To better serve the community, the embassy has created the Office of Community Affairs, which assists Salvadorans with free legal assistance concerning immigration and other legal issues or help with trade and investment, customs procedures, and social benefit projects.

The government of El Salvador also performs a very important role as a protector of the rights of Salvadorans living abroad. During the recent Summit of the Americas in Santiago, Chile, both Mexico and El Salvador played active roles in the promotion and protection of human rights of all immigrants, including migrant workers and their families.

President Armando Calderón Sol and his cabinet have also expended personal effort on behalf of Salvadorans living in the United States, with particular emphasis in the area of facilitating their immigration status. As the report mentions, President Calderón Sol personally spoke to President Clinton in May 1997, and then came to this country to work on behalf of those Salvadorans who were going to lose their immigration benefits due to the passing of the 1996 immigration law. He also created a multiparty Presidential Commission, which traveled to the United States with the same mission.

The government has also included Salvadorans living in the United States in other projects that work toward the economic development of El Salvador. One of them is the Competitiveness Project, wherein a specific set of economic actors in El Salvador is brought together to reach out to emigrant counterparts. The Emigrants Cluster, as it is known, attempts to connect small and medium-sized enterprises in El Salvador with emigrant businesspeople interested in doing business in El Salvador.

Finally, we believe that the interest shown in the well-being of our immigrants by the government and the people of El Salvador is not a temporary interest. The Commission for Development, which encompasses civic, academic, and political leaders from all parties and social sectors, has the task of creating the National Plan, which will take Salvadoran society into the twenty-first century. The plan will analyze all aspects of Salvadoran life. Commission members will visit the United States to consult with Salvadorans living there to ensure that no sector of Salvadoran society is denied input into the creation of a plan that will lead the nation into the future.

Notes

This chapter was translated from Spanish by Carolyn P. Dunlap, TRPI Research Associate and Associate Instructor, Department of Spanish and Portuguese, University of Texas at Austin.

7

Relations with the Mexican Diaspora

Gustavo Mohar

D uring the past ten years Mexico has developed a systematic strategy for the establishment of closer ties with Mexicans who have lived abroad for at least three decades. The creation of the Program for Mexican Communities Living Abroad (PCME) in February of 1990, as is explained in the report, marks the beginning of this new age in which the Mexican chancellery has opened an office whose principal responsibility is to foster and coordinate cooperation with Mexico abroad.

The PCME is an example of international cooperation through which Mexico tries to contribute to the betterment of the standard of living of Mexicans who live in the United States. It exists because the chancellery assumes that Mexicans who live in the United States are not only a source of support for Mexico, but also a brick in its wall of solidarity. One of the greatest deficiencies of the study is that it virtually ignores the initiatives of the PCME that have strong social content, those that are directed primarily to the most vulnerable sectors of the community, those related to education, health, sports promotion, and community organization.

Helping people of Mexican origin who live outside of Mexico is an end in itself. Such assistance cannot be explained simply as an attempt to keep the flow of remittances coming, nor as an effort to construct a supposed *ethnic lobby* that, given the very nature of the bilateral relation, would not be very feasible to establish.

According to the U.S. Bureau of the Census, in March of 1997 there were an estimated 18.79 million people in the United States who identified themselves as being of Mexican origin. Of these, 7.01 million were born in Mexico (U.S. Bureau of the Census 1998). The 1986 Immigration Reform and Control Act (also known as the Simpson-Rodino Law) contributed in an important way to highlighting the visibility and presence of these communities by providing amnesty to 2.3 million Mexican immigrants.[1]

Thus, the simple volume of immigrant flows obligated the Mexican government to create novel strategies (such as the PCME) to strengthen its capacity to protect its nationals in the exterior and to confront binational problems (in matters of health and education principally) that do not respect political boundaries (AIDS and tuberculosis are excellent examples). As the report points outs, the families of the immense number of Mexicans who live in the United States are the first to demand effective action from the Mexican government to defend the interests of family members who live abroad, as they correctly perceive this task as being one of the fundamental responsibilities of the state. Furthermore, since the mid-1980s, when Mexico opened its domestic market in order to make the export sector the engine of its development, the Mexican-origin population in the United States has acquired greater potential relevance, as much as a source of foreign investment as an important market for Mexican products.

Given the economic marginality of the people of Mexican origin in the United States, it is understandable that projects sponsored by the Mexican government have strong social content. To a great extent, the legitimacy of PCME strategies for establishing closer ties with Mexicans abroad rests on the state's goal of supporting those communities through education, health, sports, community development, and cultural promotion initiatives. Mexico contributes to the self-esteem and standard of living of Mexicans in the United States by, for example, sending Mexican teachers to schools that have a deficit of bilingual teachers, donating textbooks, creating Spanish literacy circles, identifying native clubs, sponsoring infrastructure development in Mexican communities by native clubs, and organizing Mexican American youth meetings in Mexico and community sporting events. Thus it is misleading to examine Mexico's efforts to strengthen ties with Mexicans abroad from a utilitarian point of view, in which the real objectives of the strategy are considered to be, on the one hand, to create an *ethnic lobby* in the United States that promotes Mexican interests in its relations with the United States, and, on the other, to promote the continuing dispatch of economic resources to Mexico.

On the economic front, without diminishing in any way the importance of remittances in Mexico's development (in the mid-1990s, they represented 57 percent of the value of foreign investment and 5 percent of the income generated by exports), often their impact is exaggerated. Their effects are concentrated in 100 municipalities in the west-central and northern regions of the country, and their relative importance continues to decrease in the national accounts, to the extent that the country has diversified its sources of capital, thanks to the growth of income through exports and through direct foreign investment. If there had been a causal or unidirectional relationship between the importance of the remittances for the development of the country and the strategy of strengthening ties with Mexicans in the United States, the latter, far from getting stronger, as has happened, would have weakened (Secretaría de Relaciones Exteriores 1997).

In the political arena, Mexico intends over the long term to exercise a positive influence on the process of identity formation of the second and succeeding generations in the United States with the objective of facilitating, however possible, the maintenance of ties that unite the Mexican-origin population in the United States with the homeland. Mexican legislators amended the Constitution to allow the voluntary acquisition of another nationality for a reason, and this amendment does not necessarily imply the loss of Mexican nationality. Certainly, to the extent that Mexican-origin communities strengthen their ability to influence the decision-making process in the United States (something that is natural to hope for, given their growth and the inclination of the U.S. political system to encourage political participation along ethnic lines), Mexico will strengthen its ability to engage in dialogue with its neighbor to the north. Most people of Mexican origin in the United States recognize that the loyalty that links them to that nation does not conflict with their desire to conserve the ties that bind them to the nation and the culture of their origin. This cultural inheritance shared by Mexicans on both sides of the border has served, and will increasingly serve, as a source of union and understanding.

The preceding should not be extrapolated too far, however. The Mexican government recognizes that, given the complexity of bilateral relations, the line that divides internal from external matters is extremely tenuous (the *intermestic*[2] characteristic of the relationship). It is natural to hope that there are important divergences between the interests of Mexico (according to how these interests are defined by the government) and the Mexican American communities, which are divided by differences of social status, geographic location, generation, and so on. The principal characteristic of these populations is their heterogeneity. It would be irrational to hope for unity of interests or points of view vis-à-vis their country of origin concerning short-term policies that would have a different effect on the population residing in Mexico.

The challenge is to identify those areas of common interest for Mexicans on both sides of the border and to learn to respect the understandable differences between both groups. The temptation some candidates in the United States feel to exploit stereotypes that work to the detriment of Mexican immigrants, for example, with propositions that present apocalyptic and inexact visions of the consequences of Mexican migration to this country affects Mexico's interests and those of practically all Latino-origin peoples in the United States, because these stereotypes give rise to a climate of hostility. That hostility affects anyone in the United States with a Latino last name, regardless of nationality or immigration status. Speaking as a voice of moderation in the U.S. debate, people of Mexican origin better serve the interests of both countries because their fundamental loyalty to the United States has never been called into question.[3]

Many obstacles remain to be overcome, as the report points out. One of these is the culture of *pochismo*, or a misunderstanding of the immigration problem. In this area, however, we must first recognize that the economic opening and globalization have had a very important impact on the mentality of Mexicans with respect to the exterior. *Pochismo* is common to the postwar period what has been more precisely called in Mexico the period of stabilizing development. It has been during this period that Mexico has *focused inwardly,* toward its internal market, in order to promote economic growth. Since 1985, with Mexico's entrance to the GATT, the model has turned 180 degrees. Now it is hoped that exports and foreign investment (in other words, interaction with the exterior) are the principal engines of growth. Thus it is undeniable that public perceptions in Mexico of those who emigrate have changed and continue to do so to the point that there now exists greater plurality and tolerance.

Notes

This chapter was translated from Spanish by Carolyn P. Dunlap, TRPI Research Associate and Associate Instructor, Department of Spanish and Portuguese, University of Texas at Austin.

1. It is estimated that probably by the year 2010, the population of Mexican origin in the United States will be equivalent to 22 percent of the population of Mexico, 33 percent by the year 2030, and 44.3 percent by the year 2050. In relation to the total U.S. population, the Mexican-origin population will be 8.5 percent in 2010, 13.4 percent in 2030, and 18 percent in 2050. See Roger Díaz de Cossío, Graciela Orozco, and Esther González. 1997. *The Mexicans in the United States.* Mexico City: SITESA.

2. Refers to issues that are simultaneously domestic and international.

3. Editors' note: As is noted in the introduction, Mexican American loyalty has been intermittently questioned since the 1890s.

References

Secretaría de Relaciones Exteriores. Commission on Immigration Reform. 1997. *Estudio binacional México-Estados Unidos sobre migración.* Mexico City: Secretaría de Relaciones Exteriores.

U.S. Bureau of the Census. 1998. *March 1997 Current Population Survey.* Washington, D.C.: U.S. Government Printing Office.

PART IV

LATINOS AS AN ETHNIC LOBBY: U.S. PERSPECTIVES

8

The Latino Foreign Policy Lobby

Peter Hakim and Carlos A. Rosales

In considering the role of U.S. Latinos (or Latin-American Americans) in U.S.–Latin American relations, as well as in broader international affairs, three questions stand out. First, what influence does the Hispanic American community have in shaping and implementing U.S. foreign policy—and is this influence growing? Second, should Hispanic Americans have any special influence on foreign policy? If so, what should the nature and extent of that influence be? And third, if a greater international role for Hispanic Americans is appropriate, what can and should be done to achieve it?

The answer to the first question is relatively straightforward. Leaving aside for a moment the case of the Cuban American community and its continuing substantial impact on U.S. policy toward Cuba, the Hispanic American community exerts almost no systematic influence on U.S.–Latin American relations or, for that matter, on U.S. foreign policy in general. An examination of several recent cases is instructive. While the Clinton administration certainly sought the support of Mexican Americans when the North American Free Trade Agreement (NAFTA) was sent to Congress for approval, no one has suggested that their support or opposition was very critical to the outcome.[1] Similarly, the Mexican American community played virtually no role in the discussions around the $20 billion bailout package the administration assembled for Mexico after the peso crisis of 1995. Nor have U.S. Hispanics had a significant presence in the debates over whether or not the United States should extend the benefits of NAFTA to Central America and the Caribbean ("NAFTA parity," or Caribbean Basin Initiative [CBI] enhancement legislation). Neither have U.S. Latinos played any role in the formulation of U.S. responses to this year's economic turmoil in South America.

Despite the large Dominican migrant population in New York City, U.S. Latinos, particularly those of Dominican descent, were not called on to participate in the U.S. reactions to the rampant electoral fraud in the Dominican Republic's 1994 presidential elections. Nor did Colombian Americans or other Hispanic Americans have much say in Washington's decision to decertify Colombia in 1997 and 1998. None of these communities were consulted by U.S. officialdom.

Although Central American immigrants send back to their home countries five or six times more in remittances than the United States provides in development assistance, Central Americans in the United States did not have a significant role to play in the U.S. humanitarian response to the region following the devastation caused by Hurricane Mitch in the fall of 1998. Nor did they have much of a role in mobilizing the necessary support to gain congressional approval of the recent legislation that authorized some $1 billion for Central American recovery.

The lack of Hispanic American influence on U.S. foreign policy toward Latin America can largely be traced to one factor—the absence of any significant organized effort to gain and exert such influence. Just like the Jewish community with regard to Israel, the Cuban American community has been influential because it achieved a significant level of organization even before the establishment of the powerful Cuban American National Foundation in 1982. The foundation—under the skilled and single-minded leadership of the late Jorge Mas-Canosa—has exercised a virtual veto over Washington's actions toward Cuba. Haitian Americans were able to apply some pressure on Washington to help restore Aristide to power because the Congressional Black Caucus, which decided to take an active part in lobbying on this issue, supported them.

The Hispanic Caucus in Congress plays a very limited foreign policy role.[2] Like the major Hispanic American organizations—the National Council of La Raza, the Mexican American Legal Defense and Education Fund, the National Association of Latino Elected Officials, and others—the Hispanic Caucus focuses mainly on migration issues and other domestic concerns to Hispanic U.S. citizens and residents. These organizations are all influential in those areas to which they give priority, but foreign affairs is not among those. Hispanic Americans can and do exert considerable political influence—despite their relative poverty and low education levels, despite the large numbers of them who are not citizens, despite language and cultural barriers, and despite overt discrimination.[3] These are all obstacles that can be overcome, but only through organized effort. Until now, international affairs have not been an important enough area for most Hispanic Americans to make that effort.

The U.S. government's 1997 enactment of restrictive immigration policies, however, helped shift immigration issues to the center of U.S.–Latin American relations. The most significant element of the Latin American and Caribbean response to the new laws is the relationship these governments are developing with their migrant communities in the United States. These countries are becoming increasingly aware of the potential role of the U.S. Hispanic community as a political ally. The relationship between the Latin American governments and their migrant communities in the United States will be a defining element in the future of inter-American relations. This will be reinforced by the growing demographic and political importance of the U.S. Hispanic community

Aside from issues that directly affect them—like migration—it is hard to know what might change the focus of Hispanic Americans and lead them, as a community, to assign greater significance to events overseas. There is nothing immediately apparent on the international horizon that will galvanize their attention. Indeed, the best guess is that this is a community that will remain very much focused on domestic issues for some time to come. Hispanic Americans, in short, are just like most other Americans—which is the principal conclusion of this entire study. Not surprisingly, they are attentive to foreign affairs issues to the extent that those issues affect their interests.

None of this means that U.S. Latinos should be excluded from the foreign policy arena. Indeed, year by year, more Hispanic Americans are taking on vital roles in international affairs. As U.S. Representative to the United Nations, Bill Richardson was the most prominent U.S. Latino involved in international issues just a few years ago. There are now many others, far too numerous to mention, in senior foreign policy positions in the White House, State Department, Treasury, and Pentagon. Equally important, several Hispanic members of Congress are exerting increasingly visible influence on international issues, and Hispanic Americans are also assuming key posts in private businesses and banks and other nongovernmental organizations (NGOs)—which are taking on increasing importance in global and regional affairs. As might be expected, the numbers and influence of Hispanic Americans are growing particularly rapidly in government agencies and private institutions whose activities are mainly directed toward Latin America. Indeed, it is almost certain that the senior leadership of these agencies and institutions will soon be dominated by Hispanic Americans. Will this mean any substantial change in their objectives, operations, or performance? Most likely not.

Notes

1. Hispanic allies of the Clinton administration in the NAFTA debate included the National Council of La Raza (NCLR) and the U.S. Hispanic Chamber of Commerce. See "Kantor, Brown Court NAACP, Hispanic Group Alleges Anti-NAFTA Racism," *U.S.–Mexico Free Trade Reporter* 2, no. 24 (June 14, 1993): 2. See also Isaac Cohen, "El surgimiento de los hispanos," *Nueva Sociedad*, no. 127 (September/October 1993).

2. Despite assurances of "commonality of interests" between members of the Congressional Hispanic Caucus and Latin American diplomats, no systematic effort has ever been made by either to work together on issues affecting U.S.–Latin American relations. At the first-ever policy exchange between caucus members and Latin American diplomats, Rep. Xavier Becerra (D–CA) defended the caucus's position against fast-track authority, arguing that "the only arguments we ever heard on this issue came from our constituencies" (luncheon discussion with members of the Congressional Hispanic Caucus and Latin American ambassadors, Washington, D.C., April 1, 1998, organized by the Inter-American Dialogue). Issues discussed at the meeting included key themes in the U.S.–Latin American agenda, such as trade, foreign assistance, CBI parity, immigration, and drug certification.

3. U.S. Latinos are the fastest-growing group in the country. According to the 1990 census, they number about 30 million, or 15 percent of the population. The census predicts a 75 percent rise by 2015, and the figure is expected to rise to 96 million by 2050. The current breakdown is roughly 63 percent Mexican, 12 percent Puerto Rican, 8 percent Cuban, 12 percent Central American, and 5 percent Dominican. The poverty rates for Hispanic Americans are higher than for African Americans and their education levels are lower.

9
Bienvenidos:
Latinos and Hemispheric Policy

Peter F. Romero

U.S. security and well-being are more closely tied to the nations of the Western Hemisphere than to any other region of the world. Geographic proximity, migration and demographics, information technology, and trade and transportation are bringing about de facto integration at a rate that would have been simply unimaginable a decade ago.

In recognition and support of these trends, numerous presidential trips to Latin America and the Caribbean and the Summit experiences of Miami and Santiago have produced a historic common agenda for the region—one that reflects converging values in democracy, human rights, economics, and environment. To date, the United States has been the leader in implementing this agenda by shaping policies that seek to better the lives of U.S. citizens and of the citizens of the Americas.

Increasingly, however, the strict demarcation between the interests of U.S. citizens and those of other hemispheric nations is blurring as a result of migration and demographics. Population experts predict that by 2025, more than one-fifth of all children born in the United States will be of Hispanic descent, and Hispanics will compose the single largest minority group in the United States. Although it is impossible to foresee or predict all of the effects this demographic shift will have on the U.S. Latin America policy, even the most casual observer should recognize that harnessing the experience and energies of U.S.-based Hispanic communities is not just a good idea—it is a priority. This bicultural and often bilingual experience represents an enormous, as yet largely untapped, resource for informing and focusing U.S. policy in the region. Effectively tapping into these communities is a major challenge for current and future administrations, as well as for U.S. political parties. Before looking at how government and civil society will approach the politics of inclusion regarding Hispanics in domestic and international policy dialogues, however, it is useful to look for a moment at regional trends that drive the immigration that presages Latino integration into mainstream U.S. society—income inequality, technology, and the quest for the good life.

In his new single entitled "Riding a Bike over Niagara Falls," Dominican pop star Juan Luis Guerra recounts the ordeal of an upper-class Latin American who is taken to a public health clinic as a result of an accident. The lack of the most elementary medical supplies and equipment and the staff's apathetic resignation to this sorry state leave the patient with the only remedy the clinic can offer—a kindly nurse who whispers that things will work out somehow. The song poignantly depicts an undeniable reality in Latin America, namely, that most new democracies and market economies in the region are still basically failing to address the entrenched income inequality that results in public health services that offer human compassion instead of modern medicine.

In a recently published study on the issue of household income inequality, the Inter-American Development Bank reports that, for a variety of historical reasons, Latin American and Caribbean societies have the greatest income and wealth distribution disparities in the world (Inter-American Development Bank 1998–1999). There are currently some 150 million Latin Americans who live on less than two dollars a day, an amount assumed to be sufficient for subsistence. If income distribution in the region were the same as the international average, poverty in Latin America and the Caribbean would be halved. If the region's income were distributed as it is in Southeast Asia, only 30 million of its inhabitants—rather than 150 million—would be living on less than two dollars a day. Without focusing here on the causes of such inequality, or the U.S. and international community's responses to this situation, it is nonetheless important to keep the income-inequality issue in mind, since several domestic policy implications flow from it.

The most important of these concerns immigration; we should assume that Latin American and Caribbean migrants will continue to come to the United States in search of jobs, even as their governments and private sectors struggle to create conditions to improve the standard of living in the region. The writer Richard Rodríguez accurately reminds us that as reporters' cameras filmed Central American victims of Hurricane Mitch, those same victims stared back through the lens with a surprisingly informed understanding of the relative luxury from which North American viewers watched the storm's devastation (Rodríguez 1999). As a result of the explosion in information technology and electronic media, even residents of rural Latin America generally have some access to radio and television and, on occasion, to computers, telephones, and more sophisticated means of information exchange. Whether through *telenovelas* or newscasts, they are becoming increasingly aware of the world beyond their *aldea* or *parcela*. And certainly residents of Latin American cities are bombarded with advertising images that depict "the good life" and material success.

The most effective method of communicating a means to expanded economic potential, however, is by word of mouth, from family and friends already in the United States. When busboys and janitors are needed for a new hotel in Los Angeles or apple growers in Washington state need laborers, Hispanic immigrants in the United States can spread the word back home via e-mail, fax, and phone, with almost instantaneous migratory consequences. Therefore, while U.S. foreign policy continues to focus on building the capacity of our hemispheric partners to raise living standards in their countries, it also recognizes that the United States' own unprecedented economic prosperity will continue to draw substantial numbers of immigrants in quest of work and expanded opportunity. We also can reasonably expect that experts on both government and civil society will continue to study the foreign policy implications of the northward flow of labor and the concurrent southerly flow of remittances. I further believe, however, that those same Latin America watchers will increasingly have to study the formal and informal activities of Hispanic émigré communities in the United States if we are to effectively incorporate their experiences in developing country-specific and broader regional hemispheric U.S. policy.

From melting pot to pressure cooker to quesadillas in Virginia, sociologists and others may still debate the validity of the "melting pot" metaphor and its applicability to the American immigration experience at the end of the twentieth century. Without entering into that debate, I would nonetheless contend that the "pressure cooker" of exclusive social and cultural conformity, which used to shape the first- and second-generation immigrant's experience of "Americanization," is a thing of the past. More and more, today's Hispanic communities, and most certainly tomorrow's Hispanic American youth, can be fully enfranchised, patriotic Americans without having to sacrifice wholesale their *hispanidad*. Several anecdotes illustrate what I consider to be an inevitable movement toward greater demographic expansion and political participation by the Hispanics in the United States.

In a recent article, *Washington Post* writer Sylvia Moreno profiled the expanding circle of activities of a Latino migrant community in and around Manassas, Virginia (not a traditional immigrant destination), and brought to light several interesting observations (Moreno 1999). Typical of family-based chain migration patterns, the overwhelmingly Mexican community members are primarily from the town of Amatitlán, in Puebla. Atypical, however, is the relatively permanent presence of this community in such a rural setting, since its members are not agricultural workers who follow regional harvests. Rather, many of these new Virginians are engaged in the construction industry, fast food work, and intracommunity entrepreneurial endeavors such as providing on-site food services that serve up quesadillas and other traditional Mexican fare to construction workers.

According to these immigrants, many of whom relocated to Manassas from oversaturated "hispanicized" cities in California, New York, and Florida, cultural assimilation is still a considerable pressure with which to be reckoned, but overt friction with the local Anglo or African American communities is becoming less of a factor. Moreno points out that between 1990 and 1996 the number of Hispanics grew by nearly 50 percent in Manassas, as well as by over 50 percent in surrounding Prince William County. According to an official from the local Building and Contractors Association, some companies are offering employees English-language instruction, and local school and health facilities are engaged in informational campaigns to publicize services and encourage community involvement. Others predict that it will not be long until Hispanics enter into public life and the election of a Hispanic official in Manassas becomes a reality.

In the small town of Dalton, Georgia, Latin American migration is giving a new twist to the Civil War concept of North meeting South. An innovative program that brings to Dalton Spanish-language educators from the University of Monterrey in Mexico and from other countries has been developed by a public-private interest called The Georgia Project (Branigan 1999). The genesis of the effort was the community's requirement to give local schools a surge capacity to handle the influx of Hispanic workers' children. Drawn by well-paying jobs in the area's carpet mills, thousands of Mexicans and Central Americans have relocated to Dalton, dramatically changing the area's demographic mix. Georgia Project officials and civic and school leaders boast of their hopes that all students, including non-Hispanics, will eventually be bilingual. Similar education projects in California and Arizona are attempting to locate Hispanic immigrants who were teachers in their native countries but who have been unable to be certified in the United States. With intensive English-language instruction, these immigrant educators are becoming a valuable resource for staffing school systems experiencing dramatic inflows of Hispanic immigrant students as their parents and families relocate away from cities and Latin barrios in search of jobs and increased opportunities.

An inevitable result of this type of demographic expansion and local communities' nontraditional responses to it is that young Hispanic immigrants and their U.S.-born offspring will increasingly feel at home abroad. They will begin to develop allegiances to U.S. cultural, social, and governmental institutions without having to sacrifice their Latin American identity or interests. In concrete terms, the fourteen-year-old son of immigrants who today switches effortlessly between the Disney Channel and Don Francisco's "Sábado gigante" will likely, in several years, be channel surfing between the local six o'clock news and Univisión's newscast. More important, we hope, he'll begin to vote. And I don't think he'll be the only one.

It's not just the vote that counts. I feel strongly that increasing engagement by U.S.-based Latino communities on both domestic and foreign policy issues will be a beneficial development. In broad terms, civic participation by any ethnic community forms the basis of our motto, "E pluribus unum," and has undoubtedly contributed to the strength of our democracy as a nation of immigrants. On a different level, however, I am mindful of the positive contributions made by organized Hispanic groups during recent policy debates on both NAFTA and Nicaraguan Adjustment and the Central American Relief Act (NACARA), as detailed in the "Family Ties and Ethnic Lobbies" study. Beyond these two examples, I believe that increasing engagement by Hispanics on traditional immigrant advocacy issues (i.e., housing, health and education services, employment, and immigration) will eventually lead to a broadening of parameters to include policies and issues affecting not just bilateral relations but the region as a whole. As the "Family Ties and Ethnic Lobbies" study indicates, there has not yet emerged a clear consensus about how different national groups will develop in terms of directing community energy or nascent lobbying influence on either bilateral or pan–Latin American issues. Certainly the experience of the active and country-specific focus of the U.S.–Cuban community offers one paradigm. My sense is that whereas Central Americans may initially focus on immigration or post-Mitch reconstruction, and Colombian communities may pay particular attention to narcotics trafficking issues, Latino communities in general will eventually go beyond the realm of the bilateral as they begin to perceive U.S. interests as being in the best interests of the region as a whole. Moreover, I think there is reason to believe that individual migrants will play an important role as citizen emissaries to the region.

At its core, U.S. foreign policy in Latin America and the Caribbean seeks to consolidate and strengthen democratic governance by helping our partners develop the institutions and structures necessary to ensure the rule of law. In so doing, we are effectively encouraging societies to address difficult law enforcement, poverty alleviation, environmental degradation, open market, and other issues in transparent and democratic ways that benefit all citizens. In many nascent democracies, there simply is no tradition of broad civic participation to deal with these issues, and the learning curve to encourage citizen engagement is steep.

Given the highly mobile nature of today's immigrant, and the well-documented and increasingly easy maintenance of family and community ties between U.S. Hispanic communities and the region, an individual migrant's integration experience can ideally become a vehicle for support of the rule of law. As migrants travel back and forth to the region and beyond traditional Hispanic enclaves in the United States, personal experiences with local, state, and federal government agencies, health and welfare agencies, and law enforcement and civil society organizations will be communicated to friends, family, and other migrants. While not all these encounters will be positive, it is not unreasonable to assume that, on balance, a picture will emerge that underscores the benefits of a democratic society dedicated to personal freedom, transparent political processes, and justice in both public and private life.

As with all human endeavor, this somewhat idealized vision of Latino integration and the propagation of common U.S. and hemispheric values by Hispanic migrants will undoubtedly be far more complex and uneven in practice. And it will take time. The underlying assumption, however, that the development and execution of U.S. foreign policy in the Americas can be a more informed, focused, and inclusive effort as a result of increasing Hispanic integration and participation, is, I believe, a valid position. And I am firmly convinced that it is in U.S. national interest to encourage this activity.

In terms of the domestic role that Hispanics can play in policy formulation, I would again note the important contributions made during the NAFTA and NACARA policy dialogues. Looking to the future, I would suggest that there are several subregional and hemispheric issues currently developing that could be advanced as a result of U.S. Latino community perspectives. Some of the most immediate involve trade and economic integration. For example, the Free Trade Area of the Americas (FTAA), an initiative launched at the 1998 Santiago Summit, is a historic effort that seeks to secure a state-of-the-art, comprehensive free trade agreement for the entire hemisphere by 2005. We believe that this effort will do a great deal to encourage current trends of expanded trade and investment opportunities, leading to increased prosperity for all of North and South America and the Caribbean. Hispanic business interests in the United States, especially small and medium-sized companies looking to do business in Latin America, have a clear interest in advancing this process.

A related issue concerns fast-track legislation, or the president's ability to submit international trade agreements to Congress for a straight up or down vote that is not subject to amendment. While the United States has played a constructive role with its Summit partners in getting the FTAA negotiations under way, in the longer term, the absence of fast track will negatively affect our ability to influence the FTAA process. Concerned Latino groups in the United States, especially those that maintain ties to private sector, "Main Street" organizations in the region, could become important interlocutors in this process. At a minimum, they would be uniquely qualified to discuss the implications of expanded hemispheric free trade both in the United States and in their home countries.

Another issue that could be of potential regional benefit to a number of Central American as well as Caribbean nations concerns the idea of offering NAFTA parity to Caribbean Basin Initiative (CBI) nations. Although the administration has strongly supported CBI parity in the past, this issue has been the subject of much discussion in government, private sector, and academic circles. Again, Hispanic groups' increased knowledge of and participation in the development of this issue can only serve to better inform the ongoing dialogue. The same can be said of the potentially protracted deliberations concerning supplemental funding for Central American and Caribbean disaster reconstruction assistance. While input from regional governments and business elites in affected countries is key, the voices of those Hispanic immigrants with ties to the region could be of great importance, especially as more immigrants become U.S. citizens.

These are by no means the only areas in which I can envision active engagement by Latino groups; however, they are indicative of the space at the foreign policy table that can and should be filled by U.S. Hispanics. As community organizations begin to channel the increasing political sophistication and clout that will inevitably stem from demographic expansion, I am confident that both public and private sector thinking about Latin America and the Caribbean will note the advantages of tapping this reserve. For our part, U.S. Hispanics should best prepare by learning about foreign policy issues, discussing these issues in the workplace and elsewhere, and getting involved when the issues so warrant. Finally, our foreign policy establishment (Departments of State, Treasury, Intelligence, etc.) needs a greater representation of Hispanic Americans. After twenty-three years of experience in the U.S. diplomatic service, I heartily recommend the work. It has been a high honor and privilege to represent my country both at home and abroad. My sincerest wish is that more Hispanics would heed the call and consider working in both Latin America and around the globe within the U.S. foreign affairs community. *Aquí te esperamos!*

References

Branigan, William. 1999. "Georgia Town Finds Ways to Cross a Language Barrier." *Washington Post* (February 27).

Inter-American Development Bank. 1998–1999. "Facing Up to Inequality in Latin America." *Economic and Social Progress in Latin America.* Washington, D.C.

Moreno, Sylvia. "A New Culture in the Old South." 1999. *Washington Post,* (March 2).

Rodríguez, Richard. 1999. "Mother Nature." *The News Hour,* Public Broadcasting System (January 11).

PART V

CONCLUSION

10

Latinos and U.S.–Latin American Relations:

Theoretical and Practical Implications

Jorge I. Domínguez

T his volume reaches two principal conclusions: first, U.S. Latinos are more concerned with domestic issues than with international problems; second, there exists extraordinary variety within the category "U.S. Latino." There is also considerable variation in the relationships between particular national communities and the U.S. government and the governments of their respective countries of origin as well as in the actions of the U.S. and respective Latin American governments concerning the U.S. Latino communities (see also Farkas and de la Garza et al. 1998).

In this chapter, I ponder possible explanations of the three kinds of variation discussed in this book and practical implications of those explanations. I argue that a structuralist explanation accounts for the relative importance of U.S. Latino communities in the public consciousness of their countries of origin. In other words, the greater the economic and demographic significance of the diaspora, the greater is the diaspora's impact on the public consciousness of the country of origin. Only Guatemala and Guatemalans seem not to have acted in a manner consistent with this generalization. I also argue that there is no general explanation for the variation in the pattern of relationships between diasporas and Latin American governments, but there is a voluntarist explanation for the change in any one Latin American government's experience and practices over time in relation to its diaspora. Presidents can change these policies, but not much happens in the absence of presidential decision. Finally, I argue that both structural and symbolic factors explain why Cuban Americans are more effective than other U.S. Latinos in affecting U.S. policy toward their country of origin. Cuban Americans have considerable social class and organizational resources and a clear symbolic cause that can be addressed only through collective action. I conclude by assessing the opportunities and disadvantages that U.S. Latino communities present for the relations between the U.S. and various Latin American governments. I argue that such communities matter in various ways for several Latin American countries, especially Mexico, the Dominican Republic, and El Salvador, among those in this study. These U.S. Latino communities play a very modest role in U.S. foreign policy but, consistent with the main findings in this study, they are likely to advance the goals of the U.S. government if and when they become involved in U.S. foreign policy.

Variation in Perceptual Significance

There is very considerable variation in public perceptions in the countries of origin about the importance and impact of specific U.S. Latino communities on these countries. At one end of the spectrum, the communities of Dominicans and Salvadorans in the United States are perceived in their countries of origin to matter greatly for the Dominican Republic and El Salvador, respectively. In these two countries, positive views of their diasporas tend to prevail; the Dominican and Salvadoran governments seek constructive relationships with their respective communities in the United States. At the other end of the spectrum, the communities of Colombians and Guatemalans seem to have a relatively low impact on public consciousness in their countries of origin. At the time of the study, governmental and nongovernmental institutions in these countries had no systematic procedures and policies to engage their diasporas in the United States. Mexico was in between. U.S. Mexican-origin peoples appear frequently in news coverage in Mexico, and the Mexican government has elaborate policies to reach out to its diaspora. On the other hand, there is low public consciousness in Mexico about the diaspora's significance and few public policies focused on the impact of the diaspora on Mexico itself.

There is a good structural explanation for this variation in perceptions: the greater the economic and demographic significance of the diaspora, the greater is the diaspora's impact on the public consciousness of the country of origin. Salvadorans and Dominicans in the United States remit very large sums of money to their countries of origin; these sums are economically significant. In the mid-1990s, Salvadoran and Dominican remittances were worth more than the value of all merchandise exports from El Salvador and the Dominican Republic. In contrast, Mexican and Colombian remittances were worth less than 5 percent of the value of merchandise exports from Mexico and Colombia. The worth of Guatemalan remittances in the mid-1990s had reached about 15 percent of the value of Guatemalan merchandise exports. The trends for remittances were noteworthy. Remittances from Dominicans and Guatemalans in the United States to their respective countries of origin had risen very rapidly from the late 1980s through the first half of the 1990s; the economic significance of these remittances for the economies of the Dominican Republic and Guatemala also increased substantially. Salvadoran remittances and their importance to El Salvador's economy were at a high plateau. Remittances from Mexicans were at a plateau, but the relative economic importance of these remittances had declined for Mexico, thanks to the rapid growth of Mexican exports. (Nonetheless, Mexican remittances in the 1990s were worth nearly $4 billion per year.) The value of remittances from Colombians, and their economic impact to Colombia, had fallen in the early 1990s compared to the late 1980s (de la Garza, Orozco, and Baraona 1997, 3, 6; Meyers 1998).

A related explanation focuses on the size of the diaspora in the United States relative to the population in the country of origin. As table 3.6 in the study makes clear, the Salvadoran diaspora was by far the largest according to this measure, followed by the Mexican and Dominican diasporas in that order, then Guatemala, and, last, Colombia. The relative demographic impact of the Salvadoran and Dominican communities for their countries of origin was also rising the fastest.

These two measures help explain the variation found in the study with regard to perceptions of the diasporas in the home countries. The Salvadoran and Dominican diasporas are demographically and economically significant for El Salvador and the Dominican Republic and are accurately perceived to be so in their home countries. Similarly, the Colombian diaspora was not so important, either demographically or economically. The Mexican case ranks at an intermediate point precisely because the indicators yield mixed results. The sums involved were large, but their economic significance for the Mexican economy declined in the 1990s. As Gustavo Mohar suggests in his chapter in this volume, social and demographic aspects may have mattered more. The Mexican government, and many Mexicans, cared about its diaspora in the United States because it was so large and because it extended the social ties and meanings of the Mexican nation.

The Guatemalan case is a bit puzzling, however. The economic and demographic significance for Guatemala of its diaspora in the United States is lower than it is for El Salvador and the Dominican Republic. But it is appreciably higher than it is for Colombia. And the objective importance of the Guatemalan diaspora is growing faster than any other diaspora except the Dominican Republic's. Consider the contrast with Colombia, which the Guatemalan case most resembles at the perceptual level (though the Guatemalan diaspora is objectively more important to Guatemala than the Colombian diaspora is for Colombia). As Fernando Cepeda Ulloa notes in this volume, there are other good reasons in addition to those under analysis for the observations in this study regarding the Colombian case. And yet, Cepeda Ulloa documents a number of steps that the Colombian government has taken to reach out to its diaspora, including dual nationality and the right to vote in some national elections. The Colombian government has also created a Program for the Promotion of Colombian Communities Abroad. Similarly, the Guatemalan diaspora is more economically significant for Guatemala than the Mexican diaspora came to be for Mexico in the 1990s, yet there is simply no Guatemalan equivalent to the extensive Mexican government programs toward its diaspora to which Mohar alludes in his chapter. The Guatemalan government and the wider Guatemalan political system have done remarkably little to reach out to the Guatemalan diaspora.

In short, other factors must be at play to sever the connection between Guatemala and its diaspora. No doubt the duration and severity of the civil war, which ended only in 1996, is one such explanation. Perhaps Guatemalans across national boundaries will construct in the first decade of the twenty-first century the friendlier and more constructive relations that Salvadorans in El Salvador and the diaspora built after the conclusion of that country's civil war in 1992. As a practical matter, however, this is of importance for Guatemalans no matter where they may be, and for those who care about Guatemala's prospects.

Variation in Latin American Government Policies

There is also much variation in the policies pursued by various Latin American governments toward their respective diasporas. This variation was evident across countries and diasporas as well as across time. In table 10.1, I present an approximation of the attitudes that Latin American governments held toward their diasporas in the United States, and vice versa, around 1990. The governments of El Salvador and Guatemala were engaged in brutal and prolonged civil wars. These wars were the origin of the massive northward emigration from these countries. Many Salvadorans and Guatemalans sought refugee status or political asylum in the United States, and a great many considered themselves refugees, even if the U.S. government had not accorded them that legal status. Consequently, the Guatemalan and Salvadoran governments viewed the emigrants with suspicion or hostility. Thus both cases are categorized as negative/negative.

In contrast, the relationship between the Dominican Republic and the Dominican diaspora was already positive, although the Dominican government of President Joaquín Balaguer had not developed an active network of contacts. The Colombian case can be situated in the same cell. As the study shows, the very few actions of the Colombian government toward the diaspora were positive; the actions of groups in the Colombian diaspora were favorable to the Colombian government even if they were uncoordinated.

The Mexican case is in a category by itself. By 1990, the government of President Carlos Salinas de Gortari was already reaching out to the Mexican diaspora and, as this study notes, designing an elaborate new program to provide contacts with, and services to, the diaspora. The government of President Ernesto Zedillo continued and deepened these policies. Yet, as both the study and Mohar's comments indicate, the Mexican community in the United States remained suspicious of the Mexican government, though perhaps one long-term consequence of the new, proactive Mexican government policies may be to change how it is perceived within the diaspora.

Table 10.1 does not portray accurately the relationship between the government of El Salvador and its diaspora by the late 1990s. El Salvador had moved to the positive/positive cell. The Dominican government of President Leonel

Table 10.1: Governments and Diasporas: Attitudes toward Each Other circa 1990

	U.S. Latino group view of Latin American government	
	Positive	Negative
Latin American government's view of its diaspora		
Positive	Dominican Republic, Colombia	
Negative	Mexico	El Salvador, Guatemala

Table 10.2: Governments and Diasporas:
Attitudes toward Each Other circa 2000

		U.S. Latino group view of Latin American government	
Latin American government's view of its diaspora		Positive	Negative
Positive	Interactive	Dominican Republic, El Salvador,	
	Weak Ties	Colombia	
Negative		Mexico	Guatemala

Fernández reached out quite consciously toward the diaspora, at least in part because Fernández himself lived for many years in New York City. table 10.2 classifies these relationships as the twenty-first century begins.

There are no persuasive general explanations for the cross-country variation. As already noted, civil war was one reason for the emigration of Salvadorans and Guatemalans, and one explanation for the strongly and mutually held negative attitudes between these diasporas and the governments of their countries of origin through the end of the 1980s. But Colombia had also suffered from extensive political violence for decades, and there had been two Communist insurgent movements active since the 1960s. Some Colombians emigrated to escape the violence. Yet, as Fernando Cepeda Ulloa notes in his chapter, most of these Colombians did not think of themselves as refugees escaping their government, even if many may have had a low opinion of various Colombian governments. As both the study and Cepeda Ulloa make clear, the positive and mutually held feelings among Colombia, its government, and its diaspora, despite a very low level of interaction, are puzzling. They even include positive feelings toward Colombians convicted of crimes and held in U.S. jails. The fact of a brutal civil war cannot explain, therefore, why Colombians express relatively positive feelings while Salvadorans and Guatemalans did not. Similarly, the end of the civil war explains why reconciliation has occurred among Salvadorans. But the Colombian civil war has not ended, yet positive feelings remain. And Salvadorans moved toward reconciliation and intense interactions much more quickly and effectively than did Guatemalans after the end of the civil war in Guatemala, suggesting again that factors beyond civil war tear at Guatemala's social fabric.

Around 1990, there were also no clear explanations for the difference in government policies toward the diasporas. The Mexican government had turned toward positive attitudes and policies as a result of a presidential decision. In the Dominican and Colombian cases, however, there was no comparably strong and decisive presidential leadership; although relations with the diaspora were positive, the governments of both of these countries had done relatively little to nurture them. Ten years later, presidential leadership had become an important explanation for the pattern of government actions. Presidents Salinas and Zedillo in Mexico and President Fernández in the Dominican Republic clearly turned their governments toward a policy of amity and cooperation. The lack of change in Guatemala, and the continuing low-intensity ties in Colombia, may be explained in part as the lack of clear presidential direction.

In El Salvador, more dramatically, President Alfredo Cristiani's policies of peacemaking in the civil war helped establish greater rapport with the diaspora. As the chapter on Salvadoran government policies indicates, his successor, President Armando Calderón Sol, made it his policy to support Salvadorans who resided in the United States, even if their entry had been illegal. In May 1997, Salvadoran President Calderón Sol personally spoke to President Clinton about the adverse effects of the 1996 immigration law on Salvadorans living in the United States. President Calderón Sol created a multiparty presidential commission to visit the United States to lobby on behalf of these Salvadorans, and he visited the United States to the same end. Moreover, the Calderón Sol government's economic strategies consulted with Salvadoran diaspora business executives during the planning process in an extraordinary level of professional engagement.

In short, there is a voluntarist explanation for intertemporal change: presidents act to turn around policies toward the diaspora. The results wherever this has occurred have been positive for both the countries of origin and the diasporas. Such relations contribute to family reunification, the extension of the bonds of meaning and solidarity of a national community, reconciliation in once deeply divided societies, the provision of some protection and social services, and the transference of remittances. In the absence of presidential initiative, little happened even if attitudes could still be positive. It would be eminently pragmatic for many governments to undertake similar policies, therefore, to reach a similar win-win outcome.

One final observation with regard to the actions of Latin American governments is in order. As this study shows, all the governments, even Guatemala's, have improved outreach to their diasporas from their consulates in major U.S. cities. El Salvador, the Dominican Republic, and Mexico have done the most. Yet the pattern of effectiveness of these consulates varies greatly (see table 3.11). The principal explanation for that variation seems to be the personality of the consul, underlining yet again the hypothesis that individuals in government may matter greatly in efforts to change the policies of Latin American governments toward their diasporas.

Variation in Shaping U.S. Foreign Policy

As the chapter by Hakim and Rosales makes clear, only one U.S. Latino community has had a significant impact on U.S. foreign policy, namely, the Cuban American community. This community is led, to a significant degree, by professionals, business executives, and other elites with the organizational and financial resources necessary to mount and conduct impressive political activity to shape U.S. policy toward Cuba. There is, however, one additional factor that facilitates collective action among Cuban Americans. There is a cause, a common goal, inherent in the realm of foreign policy: the overthrow of President Fidel Castro's government.

In contrast, the only comparably common issue within the foreign policy realm among other U.S. Latinos is immigration. Immigration is the one issue with important foreign policy content that is addressed by the Hispanic Caucus in the U.S. Congress, as Hakim and Rosales indicate. Yet, most immigration issues of direct pertinence to U.S. Latinos are highly individualized: How will this policy affect my friends, my family, or me? The immigration issue thus lacks the bonding or cohesive features of a joint struggle for *liberation* or the defense of the homeland, the kind of struggle that welds together in the United States the immigrant communities from Israel, Ireland, Armenia, Poland, or Lithuania. Moreover, as this study indicates, Latinos are interested in immigration perhaps because it is a foreign policy issue with high *domestic* content, and U.S. Latinos are, above all, interested in such issues.

Thus the difference between the Cubans and the other U.S. Latino groups can be explained in terms of both structural and symbolic factors. The first is the set of social class and organizational resources that make it possible for Cuban Americans to be politically active and effective in the United States; the second is the existence of a clear enemy that can be combated only through collective action. In practical terms, there are already many Mexican American professionals and business executives, but they lack a unifying foreign policy cause and are unlikely to find it. The future trajectory of other U.S. Latino groups is more likely to resemble that of Mexican Americans than of Cuban Americans.

Lobbying the U.S. government is only one possible relationship between U.S. Latinos and the U.S. government, however. There are other ways to think about the relationship between U.S. Latinos and U.S. foreign policy: What are the opportunities and disadvantages that U.S. Latino communities present for the relations between the U.S. and various Latin American governments?

Opportunities and Disadvantages: U.S. Latinos, Latin American Governments, and U.S. Foreign Policy

U.S. Latino communities give some Latin American countries a significant stake in their relations with the United States, namely, remittances. This is of great importance to the Dominican Republic and El Salvador, of rising though unacknowledged importance to Guatemala, and of importance for its absolute size though not for its relative economic weight to Mexico. Large U.S. Latino communities also create important symbolic, societal, and affective ties between some Latin American countries and a growing segment of society in the United States. This is especially the case for Mexico, El Salvador, and the Dominican Republic.

A large stake in a diaspora, moreover, could help construct bridges across the ideological and partisan divides in the countries of origin in order to *defend our people* in the United States and to continue to benefit from the bonds that exist. Mention was made of multipartisan collaboration in El Salvador to protect Salvadoran migrants from U.S. immigration law. Mexicans and Dominicans, too, reach across partisan lines to express concern for their diasporas. Even the Colombian Congress and the 1991 Constituent Assembly reached out to the Colombian diaspora. Political parties will compete for support within the diaspora, as the principal parties in all of these countries except Guatemala already do, but the defense of the diaspora and its individual members can and has become an opportunity for within-country collaboration. In El Salvador, the defense of its diaspora may have served as one of the bridges that span the great schism at the core of that country's bloody civil war.

There are hurdles, however, on the path of a Latin American government that, emulating Israel, seeks to make greater use of its diaspora in the United States. Such a country would need strong governmental and nongovernmental institutions to construct, nurture, and use new relationships, and it would need a large number of high-quality professionals to staff this work. The Dominican Republic, as Ambassador Bernardo Vega laments in his chapter, still lacks enough of both. But, as he also points out, it would be a legitimate practical goal for the Dominican Republic to seek this objective. Pending such a change, the U.S. government will not *fear* the policy of a Dominican government toward its diaspora because it will expect failure.

Suppose, however, that there are stronger institutions and greater professionalism. Ambassador Vega suggests that the Dominican Republic might emulate Mexico. Despite many problems, Mexico has stronger institutions staffed by able professionals. The stakes for Mexico are very high. There are millions of Mexican-origin people in the United States. There is a contentious relationship with the United States over migration. There is a long physical boundary crossed lawfully hundreds of millions of times every year. There is a logical extension of the North American Free Trade Agreement (NAFTA) to include not just the movement of goods and services but also the movement of peoples, as is the case in the European Union, with its one common passport. And the Mexican government already has in place a proactive and far-reaching policy toward its diaspora. The sum of these policies can advance Mexican objectives. It could also create intense friction with the United States. For example, Mexican policies to recognize the *dual nationality* of certain individuals could exacerbate political conflicts with, and within, the United States. Dual nationality is not a novelty; many European countries have had such policies for a long time. But Mexico is a physical neighbor of the United States, there are many Mexican-origin people already in the United States, and they tend to concentrate in the southwestern United States near Mexico.

None of these issues would necessarily cause conflict with the foreign policy of the United States. The United States should welcome the construction of means for strengthening democratic bonds, which these Latin American policies may foster in some Latin American countries. U.S. immigration law is based in part on family reunification, and this is one of the aims of Latin American policies. The United States has a long tradition of international business investment and international charitable activities, and this is one aspect of the transnational economic relations of these migrants. Dual nationality has not detracted from the loyalty through the ages of millions of European Americans to the United States, nor has it caused unmanageable or unusual societal, economic, or political problems.

On the other hand, these transnational ties that connect recent immigrants to their countries of origin may foster a greater volume of migrants than U.S. policy is likely to countenance, and it is likely to foster the practice of illegal migration. There is, consequently, appropriate U.S. concern over some Latin American policies and U.S. Latino practices, but the line between U.S. gains and losses is difficult to trace. Thus there is some uncertainty concerning whether the actions of Latin American governments toward their diasporas would be to the advantage of the U.S. government as well.

There should be no doubt, however, that greater involvement by U.S. Latinos with U.S. foreign policy would serve the interests of the United States well. (This is also the key point in the chapter in this volume by Acting Assistant Secretary of State Peter Romero.) In those few instances when U.S. Latinos have acted in the foreign policy realm, they have characteristically advanced U.S. foreign policy goals. Moreover, the views of U.S. Latinos in foreign policy also correspond closely to U.S. foreign policy priorities.

"We are largely populated by immigrants who turned their backs on the societies from which they came," a German-accented former U.S. secretary of state, Henry Kissinger, has said (Kissinger 1999). This study documents that U.S. Latinos are "like most Americans." At some point, they typically turned their backs on their countries of origin. Mexicans, Cubans, and most Central American migrants to the United States certainly have, and these account overwhelmingly for the Latin American–origin immigrant population in the United States.

The reconciliation between Salvadorans within El Salvador and between the Salvadoran diaspora and the Salvadoran government was a good thing. It was also a public policy objective of the United States in the 1990s: Salvadorans did both what they wanted to do and what the U.S. government wanted them to do. There is likely to be a similar convergence at some point in the future of Cuba.

At times, U.S. Latinos have advanced goals that coincide with those of the government of their country of origin. This is most notable in the case of some Mexican American groups who supported NAFTA's ratification. And yet, while the Mexican government did mobilize Mexican Americans, so too did the U.S. government. Support for NAFTA's ratification among Mexican American non-governmental organizations was clearly and closely consistent with the policy preferences of the White House. Even Cuban American lobbying against the Castro government resembles the main features of U.S. policy toward Cuba.

The most noteworthy fact about U.S. Latino lobbying of the U.S. government concerning U.S. policy toward their countries of origin is its rarity, however. In 1997, Samuel Huntington wrote about his concern regarding the erosion of a notion of "American national interests" to guide the foreign policy of the United States. One reason for such possible erosion, he noted, was the capture of chunks of U.S. foreign policy by nationally defined ethnic communities that seek to shape and control U.S. policy toward their countries of origin. In the numerous examples Huntington cites, only the Cubans among the U.S. Latinos appear to behave in this way (Huntington 1997). Whether the problem to which Huntington points should be a cause for concern remains to be determined, but if it is, U.S. Latinos are not at the root of the problem.

The principal foreign policy goals espoused by U.S. Latinos are to strengthen democracy in Latin American countries and promote international trade and investment. These are also the goals of the U.S. government toward Latin America as the millennium begins. Were U.S. Latinos to act to implement these goals, as this study notes, they would be lobbying the U.S. "like other Americans" in pursuit of legitimate goals within the United States and in advocating that the government of the United States act on its principles and in pursuit of its objectives.

Notes

1. Data from de la Garza, Orozco, and Baraona (1997), 3, 6; Meyers (1998).

References

de la Garza, Rodolfo, Manuel Orozco, and Miguel Baraona. 1997. "Binational Impact of Latino Remittances." *Policy Brief.* Claremont, Calif.: Tomás Rivera Policy Institute.

Farkas, Steve, Rodolfo de la Garza et al. 1998. *Here to Stay: The Domestic and International Priorities of Latino Leaders.* Claremont, Calif.: Public Agenda and Tomás Rivera Policy Institute.

Huntington, Samuel P. 1997. "The Erosion of American National Interests." *Foreign Affairs* (September–October):28–49.

Kissinger, Henry. 1999. "The Challenge of Change." *Bostonia* (summer): 40–47.

Meyers, Deborah Waller. 1998. "Migrant Remittances to Latin America: Reviewing the Literature." Working Paper. Washington, D.C., and Claremont, Calif.: Inter-American Dialogue and Tomás Rivera Policy Institute.

Index

Guadalajara, 59, 69
Guanajuato (Mexico), 14, 83
Guarnizo, Luis Eduardo, 110
Guatemala: civil war in, 60, 92, 150,
152; consulate, 74, 77–78; and
democracy, 56; emigration from, 44,
46–48, 60, 64, 69–70, 76–77,
150–51, 155; and Mexico, 64; and
outreach, 72
Guatemalan Chamber of Commerce.
See Central American Chamber of
Commerce
Guatemalans: diaspora of, 150; and
NGOs, 71, 86, 87; poverty rate of,
52; remittances from, 69, 88, 92,
149; repatriation of, 64
Guerra, Juan Luis, 138

Haiti, Haitian, 34, *35,* 56, 92, 114, 117,
119, 134
Hakim, Peter, 9, 12
Havana, 114
HCC. *See* Hispanic Congressional
Caucus
HCFA. *See* Hispanic Council on
Foreign Affairs
HCIR. *See* Hispanic Council on
International Relations
Here to Stay (Farkas, de la Garza), 45,
58
Hispanic: anti-immigration attitudes
towards, 3, 65–66, 88, 137; civil
rights, 10, 14, 25–27, 46, 82, 135–
137, 142; diasporas of, 4, 21, 40, 41,
58, 148; dominance in southwestern
United States, 4; foreign policy, 30,
31–33, 93; leadership, 22, 23, 25–
30, *31–34,* 39–41, 45–46, 57;
population growth of, 3, 21, 31, 48,
71, 87, 136n3, 138; youth, 139–40.
See also Latinas; Latino; Latin
American, specific nationalities
Hispanic Congressional Caucus (HCC),
10, 85, 134–35, 136n2
Hispanic Council on Foreign Affairs

(HCFA), 10
Hispanic Council on International
Relations (HCIR), 10, 79, 81
Hispanic Federation of New York, 117
hispanidad, 139–40
Holland, 65
home country: and emigrants, 6, 13, 15,
21–22, 46–47, 51, 58, 60–64, 93,
157; and ethnicity, 41, 86, 147–48
157; and Latinos, 23, 44–47, 58,
64–70, 87, 148; lobbying for, 157;
and Mexico, 127, 148
homeland. *See* home country
Houston, 76–77
human rights. *See* civil rights
Huntington, Samuel P., 4, 12, 13, 40,
41, 89, 157
Hurricane Mitch, 134, 139, 141

Ignacio Sánchez, Arturo, 110
Illinois, 51
immigration: from Columbia, 21, 46–
48, 51, 60–64, 69, 78, 105–9, 134,
152; demographics of, 48–53, 89,
115–16, 138, 140–41; and domestic
policy, 22; from Dominican
Republic, 46–48, 59–62, 72, 91,
155; and economics, 48, 139, 156;
from El Salvador, 13–14, 21, 46–48,
51, 60, 65–66, 77, 83, 121–24; from
Europe, 5, 8; and foreign policy, 22,
53; from Guatemala, 46–48, 60, 64,
69–70, 76–77, 94, 150–51, 155; and
income, *55;* from Japan, 5; and
labor force, 46, *55, 82;* law, 60, 114,
123, 135, 153, 155–156; from
Mexico, 21, 46–48, 59–63, 68,
76–77, 115, 125–26, 128;
perceptions of, 65, 66, 88, 137,
148–50; political forces of, 48; from
Puerto Rico, 8, 31, 51, 117;
undocumented, 7, 27; United States
law on, 123. *See also* emigration;
migration
Immigration Reform and Control Act of

About the Contributors

Fernando Cepeda Ulloa has a distinguished diplomatic and academic career. He served as Colombia's ambassador to the Organization of American States, Canada, the United Nations and Great Britain, and held senior positions in several cabinet ministries including the Ministries of Government and Communications. He earned his doctorate in law and political science from the National University of Colombia (1961) and has completed postgraduate work at the New School for Social Research (New York). He also has held several high-ranking administrative positions including president at the University of the Andes in Bogota where he has taught political science for twenty-three years.

Rodolfo O. de la Garza is vice president of the Tomás Rivera Policy Institute and Mike Hogg Professor of Community Affairs in the Department of Government at the University of Texas at Austin. Dr. de la Garza's publications include a six-volume series on Hispanic public opinion and political participation, the most recent of which is *Awash in the Mainstream: Latino Politics in the 1996 Election*. He has also published extensively on U.S.–Mexico relations including two recent volumes, *At the Crossroads: Mexico and U.S. Immigration Policy* and *Bridging the Border: Transforming Mexico–U.S. Relations*.

Jorge I. Domínguez is the Clarence Dillon Professor of International Affairs and director of the Center for International Affairs at Harvard University. The author of numerous journal articles and books, his recent work (with James McCann) includes *Democratizing Mexico: Public Opinion and Electoral Choices* (Johns Hopkins University Press, 1996).

Peter Hakim is president of the Inter-American Dialogue, the leading U.S. center for policy analysis and exchange on Western Hemisphere affairs. The author of a regular column for the *Christian Science Monitor,* Mr. Hakim speaks and publishes widely on U.S.–Latin American relations. He serves on boards and advisory committees for the World Bank, Inter-American Development Bank, International Center for Research on Women, Carnegie Endowment for International Peace, and Human Rights Watch/Americas.

René León was appointed Ambassador of El Salvador to the United States of America in August 1997. A graduate of the Universidad Centroamericana José Simeon Cañas (UCA) in San Salvador he earned a Master's Degree in Economics at the University of Illinois–Urbana. He has served as economic advisor to El Salvador's Chamber of Commerce and Industry and to the National Association of Private Enterprise of El Salvador (ANEP) from 1989–1991, and was also special advisor to several private sector enterprises as well as to international organizations and institutions. He was also Professor of Economics at the "Universidad Centroamericana José Simeon Cañas (UCA)" from 1984 to 1986. Prior to his appointment as the vice minister of Economy (1994–1997), he was the director of International Trade Negotiations and Economic Integration of the Ministry of Economy. He represented El Salvador in its first trade policy review session before the World Trade Organization's Trade Policy Review Body in November 1996 and was the chairperson of the FTAA Market Access Working Group and represented El Salvador in several international trade forums worldwide.

Gustavo Mohar, born in Mexico City in July 1950, studied law at the Ibero-American University and public finances at the National Autonomous University of Mexico. He has worked on bilateral and multilateral issues for the Mexican Ministry of Finance and for Petroleos Mexicanos as head of European operations. Mohar has participated in multiple Mexican delegations to international meetings and served as representative of the Mexican government to the Caribbean Development Bank and Repsol, the Spanish oil company. He has written in publications on economic integration in Latin America and on migration between Mexico and the United States. In 1994, after being special adviser at the Secretaria de Gobernacion in Mexico, he was appointed representative of that ministry at the Mexican Embassy in Washington, as minister for Migration Affairs. Since 1998, he has served as a minister for Political and Congressional Affairs at the Mexican Embassy.

Manuel Orozco teaches political science at the University of Akron, Ohio, and is a TRPI scholar. His research focuses on globalization, international relations theory, democratization, civil wars, and minority politics. His publications include "Sostenibilidad democratica en Nicaragua" *in Sostenibilidad Democratica y Cultura Politica en Centro America* (San Jose: UNA, 1999) and "Aiding Central America: Official Development Assistance to Central America" (*Relaciones Internacionales* No. 49, 3er Trimestre, 1995). Dr. Orozco also works as policy consultant for various organizations in the United States, South Africa, and Central America, developing programs in human rights and democracy-building.

Harry P. Pachon is president of the Tomás Rivera Policy Institute and the Kenan Professor of Political Studies at Pitzer College and the Claremont Graduate University. Dr. Pachon was executive director of the National Association of Latino Elected and Appointed Officials (NALEO) Educational Fund for ten years and also served as a policy analyst for the U.S. Department of Health, Education, and Welfare and as an associate staff member of the Appropriations Committee of the U.S. House of Representatives. He is currently serving on the President's Advisory Commission on Educational Excellence for Hispanic Americans (PACEEHA). He has authored numerous scholarly articles and co-authored *Mexican Americans in the United States* and *New Americans By Choice.*

Adrián D. Pantoja is a graduate student at the School of Politics and Economics at the Claremont Graduate University.

Carlos A. Rosales is Communications Secretary for the government of El Salvador. He was formerly an associate and Central America Program Director at the Inter-American Dialogue in Washington, D.C. He is the author of numerous articles on hemispheric issues and Central American politics that have been published in the United States, Canada, Peru, and Central America.

Peter F. Romero is Acting Assistant Secretary of State for Western Hemisphere Affairs. He is the highest ranking U.S.–Hispanic in the Department of State (Acting/Designate) of the new Western Hemisphere Affairs Bureau (Canada to Chile). A twenty-three-year career diplomat, he previously served inter alia as Principal Deputy Assistant Secretary, U.S. Ambassador to Ecuador, and Charge of the U.S. Embassy in San Salvador. He received the Department's prestigious Equal Employment Opportunity Award in 1998, the Baker-Wilkins Award for leadership of an overseas mission in 1993, the Walter J. Stoessel Award in recognition of his highly distinguished career, as well as several superior honor awards. Mr. Romero is on the board of Special Olympics International, the Una Chapman Cox Foundation, and is a founding member of the Hispanic Council on International Relations.

Bernardo Vega was born in Santiago, Dominican Republic, in 1938 and attended school in his country and in England. He graduated as an economist from the Wharton School of Finance of the University of Pennsylvania and is the author of more than forty books dealing with Dominican and Caribbean economics, history, and archaeology. He has taught at various Dominican universities, worked for more than fourteen years in the Central Bank of the Dominican Republic as economic advisor to the governor, member of the Monetary Board, and eventually governor of the Central Bank. He was also director general of the Museo del Hombre Dominican for five years. He is a member of the Academy of History of his country and was president of the Sociedad Dominicana de Bibliófilos. He is a regular contributor of articles for newspapers in the Dominican Republic. He served as Dominican Ambassador to the United States of America from January 1997 until July of 1999.